Book
Production
Control

David Bann is a graduate of the London College of Printing (now Communication) and a Fellow of the Institute of Paper, Printing & Publishing. He has spent his career on the production side of book publishing. He was formerly Production Director at Penguin and Rainbird and has lectured extensively on book production. He recently retired as Production Consultant from Michael O'Mara Books but still handles production for several independent publishers. He is the author of *The All New Print Production Handbook*.

Book Production Control

Second Edition

DAVID BANN

CLASS PROFESSIONAL PUBLISHING

Printing history:
First edition published 1995 by Pira International
Second edition published 2012
Class Publishing, The Exchange, Express Park, Bristol Road, Bridgwater, TA6 4RR Tel: +44 (0) 1278 427 843
Fax: +44 (0) 1278 421077
Email: post@class.co.uk

A CIP catalogue record for this book is available from the British Library

ISBN 978 1 85959 353 0 (print)
ISBN 978 1 85959 354 7 (ePub)
ISBN 978 1 85959 355 4 (mobi)

Text and cover design by Ana Bjezancevic
Edited by Anna Marx
Printed and bound by CPI Group (UK) Ltd, Croydon, CR0 4YY

Contents

Foreword

What are the main skills you need for success in book production? Confidence and leadership ability, obviously – they're a prerequisite for any successful career. Excellent technical knowledge and a thorough grounding in digital and print processes – that goes without saying. A good feel for how you achieve the right balance between 'price, service and quality' – that's an essential. An ability to act flexibly and rapidly in the midst of changing conditions and the new demands those conditions put on you – most definitely.

But all these skills mean very little without the ability to organize, control, administer, and communicate effectively to others – these abilities are the bedrock of success; fundamental and essential parts of what you need to be.

This book sets out, in a thorough and straightforward manner, how these essential skills can be acquired. In it you'll find invaluable advice on everything to do with estimating, buying, specifying, scheduling, dealing with suppliers, organizing your work and – crucially – how to work well with your colleagues in other departments and integrate the often complex work of production into the overall shape of a publishing plan.

I can think of no one better qualified than David Bann to offer insight and advice here. In a career spanning several decades, David has dealt with it all. As Production Director of Penguin Books, David had responsibility for producing millions of paperbacks annually to the tightest imaginable deadlines – well and truly a case of mastering the 'numbers game'. Equally, he has had responsibility for its production opposite – the packaging of highly illustrated, complex and expensive reference books with Rainbird. And for many years he has been the production genius behind O'Mara Books, publishers of some of the biggest-selling and most time-sensitive titles of recent years – including *Diana: Her True Story*, the second highest-selling book of the 1990s, and *William and Catherine: A Royal Wedding*, which was available in bookshops seventy-two hours after the wedding.

To imagine the administrative and organizational skills behind that career is to realize how invaluable David's advice will be. I commend this book most warmly.

John Peacock, June 2012

Introduction to the second edition

The production controller will acquire most of his or her skills by actually doing the job and being trained in-house or on training courses. This book is intended to complement such instruction by outlining the purpose and methods of all the tasks performed by the book production controller. Its scope is the work done in the production department rather than the technology of book production, although this is introduced where it impacts on the production controller's tasks.

The first edition was published in 1995 and this new edition has been completely updated to reflect the fundamental changes to the work of Production, resulting from the many advances in technology.

David Bann,
June 2012

Acknowledgements

I would like to thank Tony Crouch, Jo Rooke and Steven White for their help in checking the MS, Teresa Solomon for her advice on pre-press, the environment and co-editions and John Peacock for his foreword. Thanks also to Niki Davies, Rebecca Hirst and Richard Warner at Class Publishing. Anna Marx and Ana Bjezancevic handled the editing and design respectively.

1
PRE-PRESS

Introduction

Developments in hardware and software in recent years have significantly changed the role of Production in all the processes which precede the actual printing and binding of a book. Formerly, Production was involved throughout the pre-press processes – arranging the typesetting of a manuscript, as well as various stages of proofing. For colour reproduction, Production arranged scanning, page make-up in film and wet proofing.

Many of the tasks previously undertaken by Production are now carried out (or commissioned to outside sources) by colleagues in Editorial or Design and, for many production departments, work on a book (apart from estimating) doesn't begin until the final PDF is received, ready to proof or print.

Page layout and typesetting

Typesetting was once the responsibility of Production and was outsourced to specialist companies. Since the advent of page-layout software, the boundary between design and typesetting has become blurred. Many straightforward books are 'typeset' in-house by the editor and/or designer, using page layout applications such as InDesign and QuarkXPress.

Outside typesetters are still used, however – particularly for larger, more complex jobs, such as legal and science or medical reference books – and, being labour intensive, much of this work is carried out in countries such as India. For less complex books (e.g. novels) the publishers may send a typesetter a template for the design. When the work does go to an outside typesetter, this is sometimes controlled by Editorial or Design, rather than Production.

In some companies Production will be responsible for creating e-book files and this is covered under Technical Developments (*see* p.98).

SPINE WIDTHS

Production is required to advise Design on the spine width of covers, jackets and cases. The formula for calculating the bulk of a book block is shown on p.136. To this spine width should be added the thickness of the boards (for a hardback book), e.g. 3mm boards adds 6mm to the spine width of a jacket or case. For commonly used papers, Production often has tables of spine widths for different extents, to save calculating them each time. Where a dummy is supplied, the spine width can be measured.

Illustrations

As with typesetting, Production's role in preparing illustrations for printing is now often handled by Editorial or Design. Production will receive the final PDF with all text and illustrations in place. Illustrations are normally high-resolution digital files (300–350dpi [dots per inch] at the final image size) from the following sources:

- digital photographs;
- photographic prints, transparencies or flat artwork scanned by the designer;
- files created in Photoshop or Illustrator.

Illustration files may need retouching to improve colour, to adjust the colour gamut or CMYK reproduction, or to remove flaws. Cropping, cut-outs and combining two images to make a single image can all be done in Photoshop.

In many companies this work is done in-house and controlled by Design or Editorial. Production may become involved in arranging high-quality scanning or colour manipulation and retouching at an outside repro house. For most books, the type of scanner used by designers is adequate, but some subjects such as art, fashion or cookery may need a more expensive machine (often a drum rather than flatbed scanner) in order to achieve the best result. The same applies to work, when a particularly complex subject requires skilled retouching and the facilities are not available in-house. Again, an outside repro house would be used to retouch the image and to supply a high-res file and colour proof to the publisher to incorporate in the page layout.

See Quality Control (p.105) for details of Production's role in the checking stages for pre-press.

Proofing

Black-and-white books consisting of only type and line artwork, or with undemanding black-and-white halftones, are not usually proofed before printing. A printout of the final PDF is checked in-house by Editorial and Design and then sent to the printer with no further proof needed. High quality black-and-white photographic books are treated much in the same way as high quality colour books.

Colour books are more complex and publishers may use a number of different workflows. Some do not do any colour proofing until final PDF stage, whereas others will obtain colour proofs from repro companies as the book is being edited. Proofing before the final PDF stage allows for more than one round of colour proofs and corrections to the colour. For work that is particularly colour sensitive, contract quality proofs (usually calibrated and labelled to Fogra 39l ISO 12647) are supplied by repro houses for all the colour pages – typically high quality digital proofs (e.g. from an Epson or an Indigo).

Some companies are using in-house ink jet or laser printers for most of their colour proofing. These in-house printers do not usually have the colour management software to enable them to reproduce accurate CMYK colour to match that of the printing press, although they will give a reasonable impression and show good detail. Companies working this way would typically ask a repro house or printer to proof up contract quality digital proofs of the entire book once the whole job is at PDF stage. Where the cost of proofing is an issue, for example with a short run, the publisher may decide to dispense with contract digital proofs altogether or just proof a few sample pages. Not supplying the printer with any contract proofs is not generally recommended, as it means the printer has nothing colour accurate with which to match on press and is only able to work to the colour standards in the PDF file.

Supplying a measure – 20%, for example – of the pages of books in which the images are of a similar type is a good way of advising the publisher of the final printed colour and providing the print minder with something accurate to follow on press. A number of publishers are working this way when they are confident of the CMYK colour skills of their designers or repro houses.

Where a special colour (usually a Pantone) is used, often as a fifth colour on a five-colour jacket, a digital proof will simulate the colour but be made up of the four process colours (cyan, magenta, yellow, black). Note that this simulation is only approximate and where an absolutely accurate proof showing the Pantone colour is needed a wet proof is required (see below).

SOFT PROOFING

Soft proofing (also known as remote proofing) is being increasingly used, particularly by large publishers, but more for magazines rather than books. Instead of checking a physical colour proof, the publisher checks an electronic file on a monitor that has been calibrated to match that of the printer or repro house. Both monitors mimic the colour values that are achievable on the printing press. Such monitors are expensive and the viewing conditions (e.g. the lighting in the room) will have an effect on the accuracy of the colour.

WET PROOFS

Wet proofs (also known as press proofs) used to be the norm but are now rarely required, except for jackets and covers (*see* p.19). Wet proofs are printed in ink on the actual paper required for the job. They are produced either on a specialized proofing press or on the same printing press that will be used for the final books. Wet proofs are expensive as the costs of platemaking and readying the press are spread over a small quantity of proofs. They are also more difficult to control than digital proofs and you will often see some variation in a batch. As such, wet proofs are not often used now except for special colours, such as Rhodamine in children's books, duotones, or for special finishes on covers and jackets.

Wet proofs can also be used for blads which stands for book layout and design and is a sample section (for example sixteen pages from the book) wire-stitched into a jacket or cover – but these can now also be produced more cheaply and with reasonable colour quality by digital printing (*see* p.103).

PLOTTER PROOFS

Once the digital proofs have been approved, for colour books it is usual to have a plotter proof in order to check that the PDF file has outputted correctly through the printer's pre-press software and that everything is in the right place. Plotter proofs are low-resolution colour proofs, so cannot be used to check the colour.

As colour quality is not an issue, plotter proofs can be emailed or sent via FTP (see below), which will save the cost of making the plotter proof (and courier costs if printing abroad), as well as saving time.

COVERS / JACKETS/ SPINE BRASSES

Although rarely used for interiors, wet proofs are commonly required for covers, printed cases or jackets. There are two reasons for this: first, although the initial proof may be digital, covers and jackets often have finishes (e.g. foiling, blocking, spot UV) and the effect of these needs to be checked before the final run; second, wet proofs are often used for publicity or sales purposes and are usually required several months before publication.

Where foil blocking is required on the spines of imitation or real-cloth cases, the designer will supply a PDF, from which the binder makes the spine brass. Production may ask for a specimen case from the binder but this is becoming rare as it is expensive. A plotter proof, which can be emailed, will suffice.

PDFs

Production receives PDFs to send to the printer. A PDF, which stands for Portable Document Format, is made up of files that look like the final printed page, containing all the necessary fonts, images, etc. Despite this, the material inside a PDF has to go through another, final interpretation once turned into raster data in the printer's RIP (Raster Image Processor). Certain elements (like trap, over-print or knock-out) are interpreted at this final stage and can change – which is why it is important to check the printer's plotter proofs. PDFs can be created directly from InDesign or Quark layout documents, or by using Adobe Acrobat software.

Before Production receives the PDFs, the designer or typesetter should run a pre-flight check, which can be set to catch errors such as missing fonts or low-res images. The printer and repro house will also run some checks before printing or proofing. Your printer will be able to give you their specifications for PDFs, but these are now fairly standard.

PDFs are easy to make, but also easy to make incorrectly by choosing the wrong settings (e.g. PDFs for web are completely different to those required for print). If the wrong output settings are used, it is also possible to change the colour in the file when the PDF is created. This is why it is good practice to colour proof after PDF creation.

SENDING PDFS TO THE PRINTER

PDFs are normally sent to the printer by email or FTP (File Transfer Protocol), but sometimes on CD or DVD. In the case of colour books, the printer should also be sent the colour digital proofs, if they have already been produced by that stage. For black-and-white books, the publisher sometimes sends the printer a printout but (particularly where the book is text-only) often this is unnecessary.

When emailing, it is best to stick to files of 10Mb or less as the sender or recipient may not be able to handle bigger files. Above this size and you can use FTP (file transfer protocol) to upload and download files, when the printer or publisher has a website that can be used with FTP software (e.g. Transmit or Interarchy). It is now becoming more common to have websites that can do this without any special software (e.g. drag and drop). The users will need usernames and passwords to access these sites. Third-party websites such as MailBigFile, DropSend, Dropbox or YouSendIt can also be used. For larger files a reasonably fast broadband connection (say 10Mbps) is needed and very large files can be sent on CD or DVD. Folders containing several folders or files can be compressed to produce a single .zip file for transmission.

2
ESTIMATING
AND COSTING

The purpose of estimating

An estimate is the collation of information from several sources inside the publishing house and from outside suppliers into one document that summarizes the anticipated costs of producing a book to a given specification and quantity. It provides the information about production and other costs that enables the publisher to decide the selling price and quantity of a title. Margins are low in most publishing houses and it is therefore important to control costs carefully by analyzing them at several stages during the production of a book.

In most companies the production controller is responsible

for estimates. He or she is thereby aware of the cost implications of changes made during the production of a book, enabling Production to alert other departments immediately if decisions will make a significant difference to an existing estimate. Where estimating is a separate function within the production department, it is vital that the production controller advises the estimator when such changes occur.

Project and final estimates

Production will usually need to do two or more estimates for a title, starting with an initial project estimate before the title is contracted, an estimate once the book is going ahead and possibly a further 'final' estimate if quantity, price or specification change at a later stage. It is not necessary to re-estimate for small changes in costs as these are covered by contingency, but major increases or reductions should be flagged up via new estimates as soon as they are known.

PROJECT ESTIMATES

Production may be asked to provide an estimate for a book before it has been contracted. The purpose of this estimate is to enable the publisher to decide if the book is viable, on the basis of its likely specification and quantity. Some companies will have an estimate request form for project estimates (*see* below).

PROJECT ESTIMATE FORM

PROJECT ESTIMATE REQUEST

To:
From:
Date:

TITLE:

Pub date:

TPS:	A / B / Demy / Royal
Extent:	
Printed:	1/1 or 4/4
Plates/illus:	integrated / plate section
Paper:	
Ends:	plain / printed 1/0
Jacket/cover:	4/0 and gloss/matt laminated [and embossed / blocked / spot UV]
Advance covers?:	No / Yes - 150
Binding:	Paperback / Hardback Wibalin + J / Hardback PLC + J
Quantity:	UK Sales
	USA
	Australia
	Other foreign income
	Export

Retail price:

Notes:

At this stage, some of the information given to Production may only be approximate and items such as the extent and number of pictures may alter at a later stage if the book goes ahead. Generally it is not necessary, therefore, to carry out a full print-buying exercise (involving several suppliers) before giving the price, unless it is an unusual specification. It is usually sufficient to obtain one price from a supplier who has proved to be competitive for the type of work involved. In other cases, the book may be estimated from a scale, or a 'ball-park' figure may be given based on books with a similar specification. However, Production should be wary of giving unwritten, 'off the top of my head' figures because they may be inaccurate and it is dangerous for an editor to take an irrevocable decision based only on a rough estimate. There is often pressure to give immediate prices, and the production controller must resist this if a rough price cannot be quoted with confidence.

Before doing a project estimate for an editor, the production controller should carefully assess the estimate request to check that the specification is likely to work with the suggested retail price. Here are some points to consider:

- Is the suggested paper suitable for any illustration content?
- Is the extent economical? (*see* p.54)
- Cover/jacket finishes can add a lot to the unit cost.
- For mass-market paperbacks, colour plates make a big difference to the unit cost.

It may be necessary to estimate using different specifications and quantities in order to decide the best final specification. It is better to do this at this early stage, rather than changing a specification further down the line.

FINAL ESTIMATES

When a book has been contracted and the final specification and likely quantity is known, Production prepares a final estimate. This is based either on the prices of the chosen supplier after the print buying has been completed or on a price scale. Apart from any contingency items (*see* p.34), the final estimate should be reflected in the actual invoices received when the book is completed.

Despite the term 'final estimate' there may still be changes in the course of a book's production, such as a change in extent or revised proofs being required. If a change is significant (i.e. greater than covered in the contingency allowance) then Production should issue a revised estimate, rather than allowing the cost overrun to reach the invoice stage before being recognized. Also, if Production advise other in-house departments of extra costs *before* they are incurred, it may be possible for the extra costs to be avoided. For example, if the author wishes to make expensive changes at a late stage, Production can advise the editor how much these will cost before they are carried out, enabling he or she to decide whether the changes are essential. In some cases this may result in a decision not to make the corrections.

Estimate requests

If the title cost cannot be estimated in-house from a printer's scale, then an estimate request is sent to one or more printers. This consists of the specification (*see* Chapter 4), along with the following information:

- *Quantity*

  A run-on price should always be requested, so that the production controller can subsequently quote for different quantities without having to go back to the printer each time. However, it should be established how much below and above the given quantity the run-on rate can be used. For example, some black-and-white web printers have a run-on rate that can be used for quantities between 1,000 and 20,000 copies, whereas others will switch to a different press if the quantity is a lot higher or lower than in the original specification.

- *Packing*

  Most books are packed either in binder's parcels (usually shrink-wrapped) on pallets or in cartons on pallets if they are being shipped abroad. Although not required at this estimating stage, detailed packing instructions will have to be given to the printer when placing the order (*see* p. 84)

- *Delivery/shipping*

  The destination should be stated and also whether there is to be more than one delivery because both can affect the cost. In the case of books being produced abroad, or in the UK and being sent abroad, shipping details need to be given (*see* p.84).

- ***Extras***
  Even if Production has not, at this stage, been asked to price an imprint or language change, it is worth getting a figure to save going back to the printer later (*see* Co-editions p.88). It may be useful to have some elements (e.g. spot UV, foil blocking, embossing) shown separately, so they can be dropped if adding too much to the production cost.

Here is an example of an estimate request sent to the printer:

From:	
To:	
Title:	A Colour Book
TPS:	246 x 189mm (portrait) bleeds
Extent:	224pp
Text paper:	130gsm matt art 130 microns
Printed:	4/4
Endpapers:	2/0 (black and Pantone) on 140gsm uncoated woodfree
Case:	5/0 and matt laminated on 150 gsm gloss art
Jacket:	5/0 and matt laminated, with spot UV front and back, on 150gsm gloss art.
Board:	3mm
Binding:	Sewn in 16pp sections, separate printed endpapers, case over boards, rounded and backed, head and tailbands, jacketed
Packing:	In cartons on pallets
Quantity:	20,000 and run on
Delivery:	To Sussex, UK warehouse
Extras:	Imprint change in black to prelims pages 3 and 4, black plate change on jacket and case
	Complete black text language change and change of all five colours on case and jacket and spot UV on jacket

DUMMIES

Dummies can be ordered when sending an estimate request. Most titles do not require them, as their specification is the same as or similar to a publisher's existing titles. Dummies are requested where there is an unusual specification, particularly for novelty books. Their purpose is twofold: for the publishers to satisfy themselves that the specification and materials match what is required; and for Foreign Sales to send to possible co-edition partners, for approval of the specification.

Dummies are made by hand and are expensive to produce. Despite this, many printers will offer a reasonable number of dummies free of charge, even if the title does not go ahead (although foreign printers may charge the courier cost). The production controller should try not to abuse the offer of free dummies and ensure that dummy requests from other departments are for titles that have a reasonable chance of going ahead. Sometimes dummies are requested at a later stage when the title is definite and these can be ordered at the booking-in order stage (*see* p.80).

The supplier's estimate

When Production has sent out a specification, received estimates and selected suppliers for the book, the production controller should carefully check these against the specification before preparing the in-house estimate. Items to check in particular are the size and the materials specified. Some printers may quote based on a lower weight or inferior quality of paper because it is a stock line. It is also important to check the *validity* of the supplier's price. If the supplier is unable or unwilling to quote a valid price until the book is produced, the production controller will have to make an intelligent guess as to any likely price increase.

Printers' estimates can take many forms, ranging from a one-line email giving an all-in unit price and no specification, to a detailed quotation giving the specification in full and breaking the price down into the separate elements of production (e.g. printing text, paper, printing jackets, binding). Where a printer quotes a price without detailing the specification (usually stating that the price is based on the publisher's specification), the production controller should ask the printer to give a detailed specification before placing an order. The reason for this is to avoid ambiguity, particularly as regards materials. For example, the printer may choose to supply an 'equivalent' paper to that on the publisher's specification, but on delivery it may be found that the paper is inferior to that expected.

The estimate form

Every publisher has an in-house estimate form tailored to the particular requirements of the company. It may consist of a form on paper, a spreadsheet, or a form to be filled in on a database as part of a publishing software suite. The estimate form may only give information about the production costs or may also include editorial, design and other costs. Some will show the gross or net profit yielded by the retail price set. The following items may appear on the form.

FIXED COSTS

These are all the costs incurred before printing. They are called 'fixed' because they do not vary with the print run. They can be grouped under various subheadings, depending on the source of the information, as follows:

- *Editorial fixed costs* include:
  translation; copyediting; proofreading; indexing; permissions fees (fees paid to individuals or other publishers for use of text or pictures); and other editorial fees (e.g. picture research). Normally, Editorial will supply all this information to Production to complete the relevant part of the form.

- *Royalties*
  Where there is a royalty, there is normally an advance (advance payment against royalties), which is payable regardless of how many copies are sold. The advance is set against royalties paid (usually a percentage of either the retail price or income received). The estimate form will show the total royalties payable for the quantity being printed and therefore whether the advance will be covered on this printing. If some of the advance is not covered on the first printing, the balance is usually added to the fixed costs.

- *Design fixed costs* include:
  design fees; illustrations artwork; and jacket and/or cover artwork.

- **Production fixed costs** include:
  digital and bulk proofs, plates and make-ready
  (changing the plates on the press, setting the ink
  correctly and ensuring register).

- **Courier costs** refer to the cost of inland or foreign
  couriers in transporting material such as proofs
  and advance copies. They must not be confused
  with the freight of the manufactured books, which
  should be included in the manufacturing costs.

- **Sales promotion** can include publicity costs, such
  as advertising, author signing tours, etc., as well as
  the fees paid to booksellers for promoting titles in-
  store, either by extra discounting or displaying in a
  prominent location, or both.

Most publishers will aim to recover all the fixed costs on the
first printing, but on occasion a publisher will spread these
across more than one printing, when reprints or co-editions
are anticipated.

MANUFACTURING COSTS

These increase with the number of copies produced. As well
as the cost of a given number of copies, the run-on rate should
also be given – this enables the estimate to be revised easily
for a greater number of copies. If an estimate is revised for a
smaller quantity then the production controller should check
with the printer whether the run-on rate can be run back and,

if so, how far. Run-on rates can usually be safely used for larger quantities, although if the quantity is very much larger (e.g. 20,000 instead of 5,000) then it is also worth checking with the printer, as the larger quantity may be re-quoted on a different press and give a cheaper unit price than the smaller quantity.

Where there is more than one edition of the same book (e.g. cased and limp), there can be a separate estimate form for each edition, and the fixed costs are normally allocated to each edition in proportion to the quantity of each. Some estimate forms allow for more than one edition to appear on the same form.

CONTINGENCY

This is an allowance for unexpected extra costs, such as a jacket being redesigned at proof stage. Typical figures for contingency costs would be 2.5% or 5% of the total fixed costs. Higher percentages will be used if estimating for a title to be produced several months ahead in order to allow for paper or printing cost increases. On one title the extra costs incurred may exceed the title's contingency allowance, but on another title the allowance may not be used at all, so that it may be possible for one or more titles to meet the excess contingency costs of others.

BOOKSELLERS' DISCOUNT

The estimate form will show the booksellers' discount, which can range between 33% and 65%. The publisher will normally use an average figure, based on historical information. Most authors' contracts show two royalty rates – a percentage of the retail price for books sold at 'normal' discount and a percentage of receipts only for books sold at 'high' discount (e.g. 55% and above).

RETURNS

Booksellers usually have the right to return any unsold copies for a full credit within a specified period, unless the sale was done as a firm deal. The publisher will have an average percentage of returns and this is shown on the estimate as a reduction in the quantity of books sold.

DISTRIBUTION AND STORAGE COSTS

Warehouses charge publishers a percentage of the wholesale price (i.e. the retail price less the discount given) for distribution, and the estimate will take account of this. Storage costs charged are normally added to the publisher's overheads.

PROFIT/OVERHEADS

Deducting all the costs of a book from the income it generates will give a gross profit figure – not a net profit, as all the publisher's overhead costs have to be covered, including salaries, rent, power costs, IT costs, etc. Sometimes the publisher will express these as a percentage to be added to the total costs of a book, meaning that the amount left after costs and overheads are deducted from income will be the net profit.

Costing

This is the recording of costs incurred and consists of a summation of all invoices divided by the number of copies actually printed, thereby producing a unit cost. This cost is then compared with the estimated unit cost and discrepancies noted and explained.

As with estimating, costing methods differ from one publisher to another. In many companies, costing is a function of Accounts rather than of Production.

AUTHORIZATION OF INVOICES AND CODING

Even when the actual costing is performed by Accounts, Production is still required to authorize the invoices. The invoice is compared with the supplier's estimate or scale and allowance made for the actual quantity produced. There may also be extra charges, some of which will have been advised and authorized previously. Where there are extras not previously advised, Production may need to contact the supplier for a breakdown or justification of the cost.

Whether costing is done by Production or Accounts, it is usual to classify the different operations under code numbers. These can represent broad headings (such as fixed costs and manufacturing costs), be specific to departments (e.g. Editorial costs, Design costs, etc.) or stand for every separate operation on the estimate form (e.g. proofing, printing, etc.). Coding is useful because when Accounts are costing they may not have the technical knowledge to classify a description on a supplier's invoice, and also because it enables costs to be grouped together, so that overruns in specific areas can be identified and remedial action taken where necessary.

Many costing systems set an 'acceptable' difference between the estimated and actual costs. This could be 5%, for example, so that costs that vary by more than 5% from the estimate are then reported and the reasons for the difference examined.

Where cost overruns occur repeatedly on specific items, Production will take account of this when preparing subsequent estimates.

3

PRINT AND PAPER BUYING

Introduction

Buying is the key function of the production department. Selecting the right suppliers will enable the publisher to get competitive printing prices and to have books and publicity material delivered on time and to the right quality standard.

Basic principles

A balance between price, quality and service is crucial in choosing a printer, but before considering these areas, the choice of suppliers must be narrowed to those capable of producing the job required.

IDENTIFYING POTENTIAL SUPPLIERS

Unlike in general printing, where there are literally thousands of suppliers capable of producing a given job, there are only a small number of printers that specialize in book production. This means that, although there are usually enough suppliers to facilitate competition, the buyer will get to know of most of them and will rarely fail to contact a good potential supplier through ignorance of their existence.

In book production, the buyer will learn to identify which printers have the right equipment for the publisher's list – i.e., presses and binding equipment that suits the quantities being printed, the quality required and the page sizes being used. The starting point is the printer's plant list and how it 'fits' with the type of book being produced by the publisher. Beyond that, the buyer will depend on past experience with suppliers, and the recommendations of colleagues in the buyer's own company and of production staff working at other publishers.

PRICE, QUALITY AND SERVICE

Having chosen a group of potential suppliers, the buyer will usually choose the one which quotes the cheapest *price*, as long as the quality and service are as good as those of the other printers quoting – there is no point in saving a few per cent on the price if the book may be delivered late or to an inferior quality standard.

Quality in book production can be defined as fitness for purpose. In mono printing of books on uncoated papers, there is very little difference between most of the printers in this market. In colour printing, however, there can be wider variations in quality owing to the type and age of the equipment as well as the skill of the operators. However, with the use of international colour standards and printers' investment in new presses, most colour printers can provide acceptable quality, except perhaps on the most critical titles such as art books.

Establishing a printer's quality standard before using them can be done by seeing samples, by recommendations from other clients or by a visit to the factory.

Service means meeting all the schedule dates and the final delivery date and, if possible, making up time if the job runs late at any stage. It also means fast answers to queries and good attention to detail. For example, where a schedule has been agreed, the printer offering good service will remind the publisher if material is not supplied on time, rather than saying nothing and putting back the date for the next stage.

The difference in service levels between printers can be dramatic and much of the production controller's time can be wasted by an inefficient supplier. When a query is not answered, a chasing email has to be sent and, if there is still no response, then this is followed by a phone call. In the meantime, the production controller will have received internal emails or phone calls chasing the information. None of this is necessary if the printer replies to queries within a reasonable time period.

Although the content of the book is the publisher's responsibility, many printers carry out checks and point out errors. This can help prevent expensive disasters. Another part of service is how a printer responds to a problem they have created – reacting promptly and admitting responsibility if justified.

ONE-STOP SHOPPING?

The production controller can choose to have all the operations carried out at one supplier or to use separate suppliers for text printing, jacket printing and binding, as well as supplying the paper. With the tight schedules that are now the norm, and the fact that publishing staff are usually under pressure, there is a lot to be said for issuing one order and leaving the supplier to coordinate all the operations, as long as the prices are near to what can be obtained by using several sources.

THE PRINTER'S SALESPERSON

Printers' sales staff (or 'reps') can vary enormously in ability. The good ones will start with a letter or email outlining their company's facilities and follow up with a phone call to make an appointment. After quoting, they will phone to check how their prices were received. Once working for the publisher, the good salesperson will act as the client's representative in the factory and help to deal with problems.

A problem may arise when a good printer has a 'bad' salesman. Here, the buyer does not necessarily have to dispense with that printer's services if they feel that they are the right supplier for the job. When the publisher is doing a fair amount of work with a particular printer, the production controller will develop good contacts with the account controller or order clerk at the factory, and can thus maintain a good working relationship.

The buying process

SPECIFICATION

Once potential suppliers with the right equipment are identified, the next stage is to send them the specification for the title or series. In so doing it should not be necessary to send specifications to a large list of suppliers, as the production controller's experience should enable the selection of a short shortlist of three or four. It is important that the printers are supplied with a written and exact specification (as described in Chapter 4) rather than provided with the details verbally, by phone or at a meeting. If suppliers offer slightly different specifications it is difficult to draw meaningful comparisons.

COMPARISON

When the printers' estimates arrive, before comparing prices, the specifications should be checked against the original, particularly for sizes and materials. Sometimes a printer will reduce a specified size slightly to fit a machine, or will reduce paper weights to give a lower price, and this will then mean that the buyer is not comparing like with like. In comparing prices, it is worth checking whether a printer's price differs a lot (e.g. by 15% or more either way) from those of the other printers quoting (unless comparing European prices with the Far East), as this may mean that an estimating error has occurred. It is also important to check that the estimates being compared are all valid for the same period.

The comparison will show the cheapest supplier, and the buyer then has to decide whether to give the order to that supplier or to give another, more expensive supplier – who may offer better quality and/or service – the chance to meet or get nearer to the lower price.

CREDIT TERMS

The printer's estimate will usually state the credit terms required, but these can also be negotiated at the time of placing the order. Typically, printers' credit terms are sixty or ninety days, with thirty or sixty days being more usual for smaller suppliers such as repro houses or jacket printers. Obviously, where two printers offer the same price, quality and service, but one offers a longer credit period, it is in the publisher's interest to use that supplier.

When placing an initial order with a printer, a small publisher may find that they can only get thirty days' credit, or may even have to pay a percentage in advance. If the publisher particularly wants to use that supplier then it can be worth doing this, as long as the printer agrees to more favourable credit terms once the first one or two invoices have been paid on time.

CAPACITY

Any printer's capacity can vary enormously at different times of year. In trade publishing, the busiest time of year is July to October, when books are being produced for the Christmas market. This is also the time of year when printers are short-staffed because of summer holidays, and therefore prices are fairly firm. However, if the publisher wants work done between December and March, when the printers are usually a lot quieter, then much cheaper prices can often be negotiated.

PRICE SCALES

Where there is a standard product, such as mass-market paperbacks or standard-size trade hardbacks, it saves a lot of time to work on scales that cover different extents and quantities. The publisher can compare one printer's price scale with another, and place all the work covered by that scale with the chosen supplier for a year or longer. This then does away with the need for an individual estimate for every job, and means that Production can quote books immediately (often using a spreadsheet calculator), providing unit costs for different specifications rather than having to send a specification out and wait for the printer's price.

Scales are normally based on a minimum volume of work

in a fixed period, and may be agreed without obligation on either side, or form the basis of a contract between publisher and printer.

CONTRACTS

Where a large volume of work is being placed (and especially where this is done on the basis of price scales), a contract may be negotiated between the printer and publisher. This will include prices, a guaranteed minimum volume of work, validity, agreement to stock paper, and sometimes guaranteed maximum turnaround times for new books or reprints. Where the contract is for longer than a year, there may be provision for increases based possibly on inflation and/or fluctuation in prices of materials.

A contract also enables the publisher and printer to work together on systems such as electronic orders and progress control, as well as possibly expanding the working relationship to include warehousing and distribution.

Contracts ensure continuity for both parties, but it may be unwise to have a contract lasting more than two or three years, as conditions in the market may change. The publisher can then find that they are locked into a contract when other suppliers, in the meantime, have become more competitive, or new suppliers have entered the market.

Reprints

Normally, the reprint of a book will stay with the supplier of the previous printing. This avoids supplying new files to an alternative printer. However, there are circumstances where the reprint is transferred to another supplier to save time or money, or to improve quality. This applies particularly in the case of a colour book, for example where the original run was a large quantity and the reprint is a much lower run that is cheaper at a different printer (perhaps abroad), or where the first printing was produced in the Far East to save money, but the reprint is needed quickly and is transferred to a UK or European supplier to save the long shipping time, despite the extra cost.

When moving PDFs to a different printer for a reprint, another plotter proof should be requested (unless the book is just black-and-white text), so that the new printer's imposition software can be checked.

Printing abroad

Some publishers are able to source all their production in the UK, particularly when the list consists of black-and-white text-only books, where short lead times are required to meet demand. For other types of books, such as those in colour or involving an element of handwork, printing abroad (usually in Europe or the Far East) can yield very significant savings that justify the longer lead times caused by the additional shipping.

COSTS

In buying from foreign suppliers, the same basic principles apply as for UK suppliers, but there are additional considerations. In comparing a foreign supplier's price with that of a UK supplier there are extra costs that include couriers (with proofs or advance copies) and flights and hotel costs when books are seen on press. If the price quoted is CIF (Cost, Insurance and Freight) a UK port, then there will be extra costs for customs clearance and local delivery. This should be taken into account when placing the work, rather than just the quoted unit cost.

Printing in the Far East where labour costs are lower can show significant savings on certain types of work, particularly for shorter runs or books involving handwork. However, some specifications such as standard format trade hardbacks or paperbacks can be as cheap or cheaper produced in the UK on specialized equipment designed for long runs. Printing in Europe can be cheaper than the UK for sheet-fed books printed in black and white or colour.

CURRENCY

The foreign printer may quote in pounds sterling, in their own currency, or sometimes in a third-party currency such as US dollars. It is best to try to persuade the printer to quote in sterling to avoid higher bills resulting from fluctuations in exchange rate from the time of placing the work and payment (although of course the foreign currency may weaken against the pound). If the printer insists on payment in foreign currency and the buyer feels that it is otherwise a good deal, then the problem can be dealt with by the publisher's buying forward the currency at a fixed rate, although the bank will make a small charge for arranging this.

SERVICE

When one deals at a distance of sometimes thousands of miles, service becomes even more important. Before considering foreign suppliers for work, the publisher should find out whether the printer's factory contacts speak good English, whether it has a UK agent, whether any other UK publishers use the printer, and how long the printer has been in the export market. The publisher should also examine samples of work.

The use of emails and FTP means that distance is much less of a problem than when all film and proofs had to be sent and returned by courier, taking up to two or three days, although a courier will still be needed for digital proofs.

However, this still leaves the problem of the shipping time, which (door to door) can be four to five weeks to the UK from Far East suppliers and two to three days from European suppliers. This means that to take advantage of the (usually) much cheaper prices in the Far East, the publisher should do everything possible to ensure the schedule allows for the required shipping time.

AGENTS AND BROKERS

Some foreign printers will employ UK-based sales staff and others have UK agents paid on a commission basis. There are also print 'brokers' who act as principals – in other words, they take the order from the publisher, select the printer from a panel of printers used and then invoice the publisher (adding a percentage for overheads and profit) and pay the printer. On the face of it, it may seem a bad idea that the publisher is not dealing directly with the printer, but there are several large 'brokers' involved in book production, who have offices in the countries where the books are produced and keep a close eye on the quality being produced, often passing jobs on press. These companies, having local staff, can deal with printers who don't normally export to the UK and can often source prices cheap enough to more than compensate for the broker's commission. In addition, the broker will be able to obtain competitive prices because of the large volume of business resulting from orders from many UK publishers. A broker can also be helpful to smaller publishers who don't have experience of working with foreign suppliers.

Paper

Most small- and medium-sized publishers have paper supplied by the printer, but larger publishers will buy either some or all of their paper themselves. This may be done by the production controller or by a paper-buying department within the production department. One argument against a publisher supplying paper is that it usually has to be paid for earlier than if the printer were invoicing for it with the bound-copy invoice. Stocks also have to be maintained in case of urgent reprints and records of stocks have to be kept and checked. There can also be disputes with printers about wastage and with paper makers about defective paper. However, where the publisher buys a large volume of specific papers, the cost savings will be sufficient to outweigh these factors.

Where paper is specially made for a title, rather than coming from mill or merchant stock, there is a minimum making weight, so some shorter runs will be below this and therefore need to be switched to a stock paper. The basic principles of buying (price, quality and service) apply as much to paper as to printing, except that contracts for supply are more common with materials than with printing.

If buying paper, the publisher will have to decide whether to go directly to paper mills or to use a merchant who will negotiate deals for paper on the publisher's behalf. Publishers can also use paper management companies, who will deal with all the administration and may quote better paper prices than a printer.

Conclusion

Print buying does not lend itself to the application of hard-and-fast rules, and a good print buyer is one who has learned from experience and has an instinct for the right supplier for a particular job. The real key to effective print buying is to develop a good relationship with the printer. The way to achieve this is by continuity – in other words, by using a small group of suppliers who each get a reasonable amount of work, rather than by spreading the work thinly among a large number of suppliers.

4

THE

PRODUCTION

SPECIFICATION

Introduction

The specification is the key tool used in book production. It defines the physical attributes of the book and is then used to communicate these to printer and other departments in the publishing house. Attention to detail is a production controller's most important quality, and applying this in getting the initial specification right will avoid later problems.

The specification first takes shape when Editorial is considering a new book and informs Production how it envisages its content, appearance, size and selling price, and the market at which it is aimed. Although the initial proposal will usually come from the editor, input is also needed from Design, Marketing and Sales.

Once drawn up and agreed by other departments, the specification is used to obtain prices from suppliers. It may then be amended to reduce costs or for other reasons. When finalized, it becomes the basis for the work of all in-house departments and suppliers.

The elements of the specification are outlined below and are followed by examples of specifications for different types of book.

Trimmed page size (TPS)

This is probably the most important single item on the specification, because it determines which printing and binding machines will be used, and this has a direct bearing on the price. For example, the book may be printed on a press which can produce 32 pages of 234 × 156mm to view (64 pages per sheet). It could be that increasing the page size by only 3mm may mean that the same press can only produce 24 pages of that size to view. This would increase the number of plates, make-readies and the overall quantity of sheets printed by a third and therefore be very uneconomical. Far East printers tend to have smaller presses producing fewer pages to view.

In web printing one of the dimensions is limited by the *cut-*

off, which is the length of paper cut off with each revolution of the machine and corresponds to the circumference of the cylinder on the press. This means, for example, that a web press designed for printing Demy (216 × 135mm books) will have a maximum page width of 135mm. Any wider and the book cannot be printed on that press, any narrower and the difference is cut away as waste paper. However, the dimension not affected by the cut-off can be reduced, so a book of 198 × 135mm could be printed on a Demy press without wasting paper by using a narrower reel width for the reduced height of 198mm instead of 216mm.

In the UK, the height of the book always precedes the width, thus showing whether the book is portrait (height larger than width) or landscape (width larger than height). However, in many other countries the width is given first, so to avoid confusion it is best to state 'portrait' or 'landscape' after the size. The printer will need to know whether the book bleeds, because a slightly larger paper size will be needed to accommodate the trimming off of the illustrations. Note that bleeding is not possible on some web presses.

For black-and-white printing of long-run paperbacks and hardbacks, the following formats are commonly used:

- A format – 178 x 111mm
- B format – 198 x 129mm
- Demy – 216 x 135mm (unsewn),
  216 x 138mm (sewn)
- Royal – 234 x 153mm (unsewn),
  234 x 156mm (sewn)

The reason for the 3mm difference between the unsewn and sewn versions of Demy and Royal is that 3mm is the width of paper removed in the unsewn binding process, when cutting off the backs of the sections prior to applying the adhesive.

Some common formats for illustrated titles are:

- Crown Quarto – 246 x 189mm
- A4 – 297 x 210mm
- 'American A4' – 280 x 216mm

Extent

The total extent (i.e. number of pages – usually expressed as pp) obviously depends on the length of the copy, but in order to be economical to manufacture it is usually divisible by 16, 24 or 32pp. However, some printers have presses that don't conform to this rule, so you will need to check. Because presses (whether sheet or web) normally produce a product that can be 32, 64 or 96pp, an extent which has an odd 16pp can be uneconomical. An example would be a book printed web offset on a press that produces a 64pp section, coming off as 2 x 32pp. On this press a book of 192pp consists of 6 sections of 32pp. If it is 176pp the odd 16pp section has to be printed two-up (*see* p.56), increasing platemaking costs, so that often a printer's price for a 176pp book is actually *higher* than for a book of 192pp. Where the publisher has price scales, these will show the uneconomical extents and Production can alert Editorial and Design to these. However, there will be occasions when it is not possible to reduce or expand the text to a multiple of even 32pp sections.

Endpapers

The endpapers used on hardback books are normally on uncoated cartridge paper of around 135gsm and can be printed in one or more colours. Self-coloured endpaper material is also available, instead of printing a solid colour on white paper, but is usually costlier than printing the endpapers. It is also possible to have self-ends, where the first and last pages of the book are glued down to the case as if they were endpapers. This saves money, but creates a potential point of weakness at the 'hinge', particularly when text papers of lighter weight (80gsm or less) are used. Self-ends should only be used on thinner books (i.e. not more than 160pp).

Printing

The shorthand for the number of colours on each side of the sheet is 1/1 (black and white throughout), 4/4 (four colour throughout) and so on for different combinations. For 2/2 printing, this is often black and a Pantone. You will need to specify the Pantone number and whether it is for uncoated (U) or coated paper (C). Some colour books may have a seal, which is a varnish applied on the press that can be either gloss to make the illustrations glossy or matt to prevent marking due to ink rubbing.

Integrated illustrations and plate sections

Illustrations can appear in mono (black-and-white) books in two ways. *Integrated* halftones can appear on any page in the book, but to do this the paper will usually be higher in quality than that used for text only – usually white woodfree or matt art paper. The use of integrated illustrations may also mean that the book has to be printed sheet fed rather than web because of drying considerations, as most black-and-white web presses don't have driers, so can't use smooth papers because of set-off (smudging). Longer run colour books with integrated illustrations can be printed on colour web presses which have drying facilities.

Illustrations (either black-and-white or colour) can also appear as plates in a separate section printed on a higher quality paper (gloss or matt art) on a different printing press. They can be positioned as one or several sections (e.g. 32pp of plates as 4 × 8pp) or as wraps or inserts. A wrap is 4 or 8 pages of plates wrapped round a 16- or 32pp text section, and an insert is 4 or 8pp of plates inserted into the middle of a 16- or 32pp text section. Wraps and inserts are expensive because of the extra binding operations required, so it is more usual for plates to be bound in as separate sections.

Long run black-and-white books printed by web-offset (both paperback and hardback) are often bound two-up, meaning that the press produces a 64pp section, consisting of 2 x 32pp joined at the head, for example the first 32pp of a book joined to last 32 and so on. This means that when the sections are gathered together they produce a book block of two complete copies, which are then bound in that form and subsequently trimmed into individual copies. In this form the plate sections also have to be printed two up and there are restrictions as to where they can be positioned between text sections – the printer can advise you of these.

Paper

There are very many types of paper available but the range used in book production is usually limited to the following types, which are often held in stock by printers and paper merchants:

- **Bulky News** – this is the cheapest paper for books and is normally used for the lower cost mass-market paperbacks (e.g. crime/thrillers). It is uncoated and has a high percentage of mechanical wood, meaning that over time and exposure to light it will tend to turn yellow. A common weight is 53gsm with a high bulk (see below) of 127 microns. A whiter version is also used for higher quality books and this is often 60gsm with a bulk of 120 microns.

- **Antique Wove** – an uncoated bulky paper commonly used for trade hardback books. It can be woodfree (meaning no mechanical wood content), which is whiter and will not turn yellow over time, but more often contains a small proportion of mechanical wood. Often this paper is used in 80gsm with a bulk of 144 microns.

- **White Woodfree** – this contains no mechanical wood and, although uncoated, provides a smoother surface for halftones, as well as being whiter. This paper is not as high in bulk as Antique Wove, so 100gsm for example can have a bulk of 130 microns. Weights of this paper are usually between 80gsm and 150gsm.

- **Matt Art** – usually a woodfree paper with a smooth but matt-coated surface. It is used for books with colour or black-and-white photographs and is less bulky than other book papers – typically 130gsm matt art will be 130 microns. The reason for using matt rather than gloss art is to avoid the reflection back from the paper, which can affect the legibility of the text. Typical weights used range from 115 to 150gsm. This paper cannot be used on most black-and-white web-offset presses used for long run paperbacks and hardbacks, as the presses have no driers and the smooth surface of matt art would result in smudging. This paper can be printed on sheet-fed offset presses or colour web-offset presses with heat driers (web-offset is used for long runs).

Gloss Art – used for colour or black-and-white photographs, where there is little text. Other details are as for matt art.

BULK

The bulk of a paper is much more important for books than other forms of printing. The greater number of pages in a book than in a magazine or brochure means that increasing the bulk will have a noticeable effect on the thickness (and therefore perceived value) of the product. This means that short books are often 'bulked out' by using the thickest possible paper and sometimes also using a large typeface and wide margins to spread content over more pages. A paper's bulk can be expressed either as a Vol. (volume) figure or the thickness of the sheet in microns. *See* p.136 for the formula to convert Vol. to microns and thus calculate the thickness of the book block, so the spine width can be given.

GRAIN DIRECTION

This is the direction in which the paper is made. Ideally in books the grain of the paper should run parallel to the spine (right-grain), to enable pages to lie flat and open easily. In certain countries (e.g. Germany), publishers will not accept 'wrong-grain' binding, but unfortunately in the UK nearly all the web-offset book presses produce a 'wrong-grain' book. For books of longer extents this results in a 'brick-like' object, where the wrong grain of the paper combined with unsewn binding makes the book difficult to open and read. The reason for this is that the presses which produce wrong-grain products have much simpler folders than right-grain presses and therefore a much lower capital cost. Where books are printed by sheet-fed offset it is no problem to supply a right-grain product.

Covers/jackets/ printed cases

Covers (i.e. for paperbacks) are usually printed on one-sided art board, with a gloss- or matt-coated surface on the printed side and uncoated on the other. This is because the uncoated inner surface of the board enables better adhesion to the book block in binding. However, if the inside is required to be printed, two-sided art board can be used. The weight of board used ranges from 200gsm for mass-market paperbacks up to 350gsm for long extent books, which need stronger covers.

Jackets and *printed cases* (for hardbacks) are printed on art paper usually ranging from 135gsm to 150gsm. Most hardback books have cases made from imitation cloth with blocking on the spine, but some (particularly children's books and cookery books) have printed cases instead. Sometimes printed cases are used without a jacket and described as PLC (printed laminated case) or PPC (printed paper case). Where books have both a printed case and a printed jacket, the description is PLC/J or PPC/J. Usually the printed case has the same design as the jacket, but may be designed to omit finishes such as foil blocking, etc. (see below).

Finishes

There is a wide range of finishes available for covers and jackets and publishers are making use of these more and more to ensure their titles stand out on the booksellers' shelves. Some of these are quite expensive, but considered worthwhile if the publisher believes that their use will increase sales.

COATING

Covers and jackets are usually given some form of coating for protection. The cheapest coating is UV varnish, where a liquid varnish is applied to the printed sheet to give protection and gloss. Being the least expensive option this is often used for mass-market paperbacks, although lamination is now being used for many paperbacks. Lamination (used for nearly all hardbacks) is where a thin sheet of transparent plastic is attached with adhesive to the printed sheet. Lamination can be gloss or matt. Matt is slightly more expensive but its use is increasing. Matt lamination can tend to mark and there are more expensive versions that avoid this – for example, hard matt lamination or 'velvet' lamination, which although matt has a very smooth feel. Lamination can also be grained to give a cloth-like feel.

FOIL BLOCKING

Covers and jackets can be blocked in foil, which is often metallic (e.g. gold or silver) but may be any colour. Blocking can be matt or gloss. Holographic foils, which are patterned, are also available.

EMBOSSING/DEBOSSING

Here a pair of dies is made and the application of heat and pressure makes an indentation on the paper or board. Embossing will show a raised area and debossing an indented area. Embossing is often used in combination with foil blocking so that the foil-blocked area (often the title of the book) stands proud of the background design. Embossing/debossing is not used on printed cases, as the indentations mean that a case cannot be glued properly to the boards when case making. The same applies to the spines of paperback covers, although fronts and backs can be embossed.

SPOT UV VARNISHING

This is an increasingly common finish. It is used in combination with matt lamination, so that the area that is gloss varnished stands out from the matt background of the rest of the design. The area with spot UV can also be embossed to give it even more emphasis.

Binding

Although paperback binding (being automated) forms only a small proportion of the total production cost of a book, hardback binding is a major part of a book's cost, so Production needs to specify a binding style which is both cost-effective and suitable for the type of book in question.

UNSEWN BINDING

Paperbacks are usually unsewn (also described as 'perfect' binding), meaning that the pages are glued to each other with adhesive and the book block is affixed to the inner spine of the cover. Modern unsewn binding is quite reliable and there is rarely a problem with pages becoming detached. It is considerably cheaper than sewn binding. Many hardbacks are now also unsewn. Unsewn binding using PUR adhesive gives a more flexible spine and helps the book to lie flat when opened. Notch binding is also unsewn but the backs are not removed from the sections – instead, notches are made along the spines and these are filled with adhesive, which both holds each section together and fixes the sections to each other.

SEWN BINDING

This is where a 16-, 24- or 32-page section is held together with threads in the spine, which also join the sections of a book together. It is used for higher priced books, particularly those printed on coated paper, which is not so suitable for unsewn binding. Although a lot more expensive in the UK, sewn binding in the Far East is usually affordable and may be the only form of binding offered. In the specification Production must state the number of pages in each sewn section. For heavier papers (130gsm or higher) this should be 16 or 24 pages, but 32-page sections are acceptable for lower weight papers.

PAPERBACKS WITH FLAPS

These can be either unsewn or sewn. They are becoming more popular and some printers have binding equipment to enable them to be produced economically. The flaps protrude by 3mm from the book block, so the block must be trimmed before covering.

CASES

For hardbacks the board thickness should be specified – normally between 2mm and 3mm. 3mm is often used for thinner books in order to increase the bulk (as well as using bulky paper as described above). Cases can be covered with printed cases (see above) but more often are covered with imitation cloth (a coloured paper grained to make it look like cloth). There is a choice of grains (e.g. buckram or fine linen), which should be specified. Much more expensive books will have cases made of real cloth. Imitation or real cloth cases are foil blocked on the spine in gold, silver or other colours and the blocking shows the title, author and publisher's logo. Cases can also be foil blocked on the front, but this adds to the cost.

ROUNDING AND BACKING OR SQUARE BACK

Hardback books can have a rounded spine or flat square spine. The rounded back in the spine of the case is made from thinner board than the front and back boards, so that it is flexible enough to curve round the spine. Rounding and backing produces a stronger book as the pages are gripped together more tightly. Square-backed books have a stiff board in the spine (the same thickness as the front and back boards). Square backs are often used on children's books or cookery books, as they lay flat more easily when open.

HEAD AND TAIL BANDS

These should be specified if required, as should ribbon markers.

Packing

The correct packing specification must be given to meet the requirements of the warehouse. Packing can be in binder's parcels (usually shrink-wrapped) or cartons. Cartons are normally needed for export to prevent damage in transit. All warehouses require delivery on pallets. *See* p.84 for full details.

Shipping

Where books are being exported or imported shipping details will be needed to enable the printer to quote shipping costs. *See* p.84 for details of these.

Example specifications

B-format black-and-white paperback

TPS:	198 x 129mm (portrait), no bleeds
Extent:	448pp
Text:	1/1 on 53gsm bulky news 127 microns
Cover:	4/0, matt laminated, blocked over

	matt lamination and embossed on 240gsm 1-sided artboard
Binding:	Unsewn, limp, cover drawn on and glued, cut flush
Packing:	In binder's parcels on pallets

Royal black-and-white hardback with colour plate sections

TPS:	234 x 153mm (portrait) only plates bleed
Extent:	256pp + 16pp plates
Text paper:	80gsm Antique Wove 144 microns
Printed:	1/1
Endpapers:	Plain, on 135gsm offset cartridge
Plates:	4/4 on 130gsm gloss art
Case:	Imitation cloth, Fine Linen finish, blocked on spine in gold
Jacket:	4/0 on 130gsm 1-sided art, matt laminated, and embossed
Boards:	3mm
Binding:	Unsewn, plates as 2 x 8pp sections between pages 96 and 97 and 160/161, rounded & backed, jacketed
Packing:	In cartons on pallets

Crown quarto colour hardback with printed case and jacket

TPS:	246 x 189mm (portrait) bleeds
Extent:	224pp
Text paper:	130gsm matt art 130 microns
Printed:	4/4
Endpapers:	2/0 (black and Pantone) on 140gsm uncoated woodfree
Case:	5/0 (5th colour is Pantone) and matt laminated on 150gsm gloss art

Jacket:	5/0 (5th colour is Pantone) and matt laminated, with spot UV front and back, on 150gsm gloss art.
Board:	3mm
Binding:	Sewn in 16pp sections, separate printed endpapers, case over boards, rounded and backed, head and tailbands, jacketed
Packing:	In cartons on pallets

5
SCHEDULING

Introduction

The objectives of scheduling are to:

- deliver the book in time for publication;
- have publicity material ready when required;
- allow sufficient time for checking by the author, Editorial and Design;
- allow sufficient time for proofing, manufacturing and shipping.

Although the schedule is drawn up by the production controller, whether it is achieved depends on other departments at the publisher and on outside suppliers. A schedule is therefore an exercise in coordination and communication to enable several parties to achieve a common goal.

New book and reprint programmes

Most publishers have a provisional programme for new books up to two years ahead of publication and reprint programmes up to a few months ahead, although often reprints are only programmed on demand and at short notice. Because the information is sketchy and dates can change, the programmes are usually based on average times for producing certain types of new book or reprint, rather than on detailed schedules. The detailed schedule is not usually issued until firm dates are available for the manuscript and the cover and/or jacket design, although sometimes the publication is fixed and the schedule devised by working backwards, arriving at target dates for text file and cover and/or jacket design.

Some publishers have *standard schedules* for different types of book based on past experience, and these are applied to the individual titles to give the publication dates.

Schedule events

Assuming all pre-press processes are arranged by Editorial and Design, Production has to schedule black-and-white titles to allow for the following events:

- *Order paper (in advance unless printer holds stock paper)* – specially made paper can take a month and needs to be available at the same time as the text PDF

- *Cover/jacket PDF to proof*
- *Cover/jacket digital proofs in* – normally two to three days
- *Cover/jacket digital proofs approved* – can be up to two weeks, if checked by several departments
- *Cover/jacket wet proofs in* – two to three weeks to allow for foil blocking or other finishes. Cover/jacket wet proofs are usually required (for publicity and booksellers) up to six months before publication
- *Text PDF to printer* – usually no plotter needed on black-and-white books
- *Delivery date* – usually four to five weeks before publication to allow time for Publicity to send to reviewers. Printing and binding for black-and-white books is usually only two to three weeks (excluding freight time), although it is possible to improve on this lead-time significantly. Where a publisher has a contract with a printer, this often gives agreed maximum lead times.
- *Publication date*

For colour titles, there are the following additional events:

- *Text PDF to proof* – colour digital proofs should take two to three days
- *Text digital proofs in*
- *Text digital proofs approved* – time depends on how many in-house departments have to check them
- *Plotter proofs in* – one to two weeks after PDF

- *Plotter proofs approved* – normally two to three days as checking at this stage is just by one or two people
- *Delivery date* – printing and binding for colour books normally takes about three to four weeks (plus freight time) from approval of the plotter proof. Delays in approving a plotter proof or corrections requiring a revised plotter proof will increase the lead-time.

Shipping

Most UK printers can deliver the same day, but in some cases the distance of the publisher's warehouse from the printer means next-day delivery. When printing takes place abroad, allow two to four days for European printers and four to five weeks for the Far East.

Transit times

The schedule should make allowance for the time taken to get material to and from the supplier. The dates given in the examples are for material arriving at or leaving the publisher, meaning that it leaves the supplier on the previous working day and arrives at the supplier on the next working day. With foreign suppliers an extra day or two each way needs to be built in. This won't be required if material is sent electronically.

Holidays

In the UK and Europe, most suppliers shut completely between Christmas and New Year, and suppliers in the Far East close for up to two weeks for Chinese New Year at the end of January or early February. Other public holidays only last a day or two at a time and can usually be absorbed in the schedules.

Capacity

Peak demand for trade publishing printing and binding is August and September, when books are being delivered in time for publication in September or October for the Christmas market. This can coincide with staff summer holidays, meaning that a printer's capacity can be full or over-full at this time of year. It is therefore important that the publisher's PDF dates do not slip, as it may be difficult for the printer to make up lost time.

Co-editions

When printing a co-edition consisting of several editions in different languages, it is wise to build extra time into the schedule because at least one of the co-publishers may be late in supplying their files and thus hold up the printing of all the editions. (*See* Chapter 7 p.88 for more on co-editions).

Contingency

Where possible, Production should build a contingency (e.g. one to two weeks) into the schedule to allow for late running.

Rush titles

Where a title has to be produced very quickly, perhaps because it is topical or tied in to a particular event such as the showing of a TV programme, then it is possible to compress all the above times (except shipping, unless using expensive air-freight) and to produce a book from start to finish in a week or less if it is not illustrated and two to three weeks if it is. However, this can only be achieved if all parties concerned are alerted in advance so that the work is booked in.

Reprints

Reprints of mass-market paperbacks or web-offset hardbacks can be achieved in a week or less and, where a publisher works on a contractual price scale, maximum lead times for reprints are often specified as part of the contract. Reprints of sheet-fed books normally take two to three weeks from when paper becomes available.

Improving schedules

Where an initial schedule yields a delivery date that is too late for the required publication, or Editorial or Design dates that cannot be achieved, then the production controller should examine the schedule in detail to see how time can be saved. Rather than using the standard times for different operations, suppliers can be contacted to see if they will agree shorter times for specific operations, and if the order has not already been placed then the faster work can be made a condition of the order. Another approach is where the party responsible for a delay can make up time in the area they control (e.g. if Editorial is late with a PDF its staff may be required to check proofs faster than usual).

Where the publisher has several titles placed with a supplier, work can often be rescheduled to delay a less urgent title and advance an urgent one. Sometimes a better delivery date can be achieved by only having part of the total quantity delivered, with the balance following a few days later.

Where the publisher has a good working relationship with the printer they can work together so that on occasion the printer will produce a book more quickly than the agreed lead time and, in return, the publisher may allow a printer slightly longer where the delivery date is not crucial.

Monitoring schedules

The production controller should continually monitor the schedules to get early warning of any delays. Apart from regular *progress meetings* (see below), Production will usually have a diary or computer system to alert it to imminent dates. A diary system simply lists the events due to happen or the tasks that need completing on a given day. It is the production controller's role to check with suppliers and internal departments a day or two beforehand that the dates will be met. Ideally, suppliers will advise of delays before they occur. In large companies the schedules may be on a database that is available to all departments, and which enables the user to list all due or overdue items.

Increasingly, printers are offering publishers access to their MIS (Management Information System), which will typically show the scheduled delivery date of a title; any missing components; whether the order is awaited; what stage it has reached in production and list the delivery quantities and destinations. Some of these systems are 'read-only' but others enable the publisher to make alterations. Some systems even allow the publisher to input the order, rather than sending a separate printing and binding order (*see* p.87).

For printing and binding, a delay in supplying a PDF or ordering paper may mean that the delay in delivery is made even longer because the job has lost its allotted time or 'slot' on the machine. Where suppliers are running late, the production controller must advise the relevant colleagues immediately. Failure to advise of a delay can be worse than the delay itself, as it means that colleagues cannot take actions such as postponing publication or advising an author of lateness of proofs. No one likes to be the bearer of bad news, but this role often falls to Production, and the sooner it is performed the better.

Progress meetings

Most publishers hold regular progress meetings, where every title is reviewed to see if it is running on schedule. In a small company the size of the list means that usually every title can be reviewed at every meeting, and this can also be done if divisions of large companies have separate progress meetings. Larger companies may only be able to deal with a part of the list at each meeting.

It is important that only those who have authority to speak for their departments and to take decisions at the meeting attend the meeting, and also that people do not attend unless they are taking an active part. Minutes should be taken that list the decisions made and the action points and these should be circulated within a day or two of the meeting.

The progress meeting is not the place for one department to criticize another or to hold detailed postmortems on why things have gone wrong. If continuing delays or other problems emerge at progress meetings they should be dealt with in separate meetings.

Conclusion

Schedules can only be planned and maintained by several parties (both within the publishing house and externally) if all are working together towards a common target. The production controller's job is to act as the liaison between suppliers and colleagues. Communication is vital for the process to work.

6
ORDERS

Introduction

The order is the written confirmation of a contract between the publisher and the supplier. It should be concise, accurate and issued in good time.

This chapter deals with printing and binding orders, but orders should also be issued for reproduction and proofing work, stating the work to be done, the agreed price, the agreed proof and delivery dates, and terms. Some books will only have one order if they are produced on a scale or use stock paper. More complex titles may need orders at three stages: booking in, materials order and final order. These are necessary if the quantity is not known at the time of placing the work and if, when the paper order is placed, the detailed delivery instructions are also unknown.

Publishers all have their own order forms, which

may contain extra details specific to their own particular requirements.

Booking-in order

The purpose of this order, which may be placed before the final quantity is known, is to agree a fixed price and to book the capacity at the printer. This could simply be an email referring to the printer's estimate and giving provisional quantity and delivery dates. A blank dummy can also be ordered at this stage, if not already ordered previously.

Materials order

If the paper being used is not a stock item and the final delivery details are not known at the time the paper needs to be ordered, Production may need to issue a materials order ahead of the full printing and binding order. Again, this could be an email, with all the other details to be advised at a later date in the final printing and binding order.

Printing and binding order

This is the document that gives the printer all the final details required to complete the work. It forms the basis of a contract between publisher and printer for production of the title and therefore needs to be prepared with care and checked thoroughly.

SPECIFICATION AND PRICE

It is best to give the specification in full, unless it is a standard specification (e.g. on a price scale). As there may be more than one estimate, the number and date of the relevant one should be given. Stating the actual prices on the order means that it can be used for checking the invoice, without having to refer back to the original estimate.

QUANTITY

When giving the quantity, state the agreed tolerance: 5% is fairly standard, but lower tolerances may be agreed on long runs and higher tolerances on short ones. This is important because if the printer exceeds the tolerance then the publisher may refuse to accept the extra copies, and if there is a shortage in excess of tolerance then in extreme cases the printer may have to go back to press to make up the shortfall.

EXTRA JACKETS

For a hardback book, the publisher will often require extra trimmed, laminated jackets delivered to the warehouse. These are used for replacing damaged jackets on returned copies.

IMPRINT AND LANGUAGE CHANGES

Clear instructions should be given about imprint and language changes.

PACKING AND SHIPPING

Packing (*see* p.84) and delivery and shipping instructions (*see* p.84) should be attached.

ADVANCE COPIES

The order will also state advance copy requirements. True advance copies are hand-bound and sent for approval before binding begins. As quality standards have improved and schedules are faster, very few titles now have true advance copies. Instead, the term is used to describe copies from the run sent to the publisher as soon as they are available, to arrive a day or two before the bulk copies are delivered to the warehouse (or much longer in the case of Far East printing). Unless it is specifically requested, the printer will not await the publisher's approval of the advance copies before dispatching the bulk copies.

RUNNING SHEETS

Running sheets are usually supplied as F&Gs (folded and gathered sections). The publisher can request running sheets (usually only on colour titles) and needs to be clear whether these are for approval or just information. Where printed sheets are sent for the publisher's approval, the printer will not proceed to the next stage until they get the go-ahead.

PAYMENT TERMS

The terms of payment should be stated on the order: the length of credit terms and also if a specific payment method is being used.

AMENDMENTS

It is important to get all the information on to the printing and binding order, rather than sending through amendments and additional information later. When receiving the order, the printer's account executive will issue an internal order to several departments and if information comes through later there is a danger it will be missed.

Packing and delivery instructions

The publisher's warehouse will supply details of its requirements which should include the following:

- *Packing*: specification of shrink-wrapped parcels or cartons required (may need to be double-walled for export); number of copies and weight of packages; labelling instructions; type, size and maximum height of pallets (which may need to be fumigated).

- *Delivery*: address; phone and email; name of contact; instructions about booking in deliveries in advance; opening hours of warehouse.

It is important that the printer is given the above information clearly and in good time. Warehouses may impose fines or refuse to accept deliveries that do not conform to their requirements, which will cause delays and extra costs.

Shipping instructions

Shipping instructions for UK or foreign publishers' warehouses will normally be supplied to Production by the publisher and should contain the following information, as well as packing and delivery instructions as above:

- **Method of shipping**: this should specify Ex-Works, CIF, FOB, DDU, DDP or FDW (see below) and the name of port to be used.

- **Consignment address**: this is the actual delivery address; it is required for the documents, even if delivery is only to a port.

- **Documents**: a list of documents is required that can include: the bill of lading; insurance certificate; packing list; and proforma invoice (issued for customs purposes, stating the quantity and price).

- **Destination of documents**: the original set is usually sent to a shipping agent in the importing country and copy sets may be required by the importing publisher. (Note that the goods cannot be cleared through customs without the documents.)

SHIPPING TERMINOLOGY

Where a foreign printer is being used, or a UK printer is asked to deliver to a foreign country, the type of freight must be specified. *CIF* means cost, insurance and freight to a port – the importer then pays the cost of customs clearance and local delivery in the destination country. *Ex-works* means that the publisher will collect from the printer's factory. *FOB* is free on board at a port, with the importer being responsible for sea freight from that port as well as the customs clearance and delivery in the destination country. *FDW* means full delivery warehouse, so that the printer pays all costs through to delivery to the publisher's warehouse. *DDU* (delivery duty unpaid) is another term for this – this applies to books, as they aren't usually subject to VAT or duty. *DDP* is delivery duty paid and would be used for any novelty books or books plus, where they attract duty and/or VAT. There are obviously big differences in costs between these methods, so it is important to be clear as to which is required.

VAT and duty

Books can normally be imported from or exported to most countries without attracting VAT or duty. However, items such as diaries, address books or novelty books may attract both VAT and duty. Production should be aware of this before the work is placed because it will affect the price and may also mean switching from a foreign to a UK supplier to avoid extra costs. The VAT element can be reclaimed for the import, but will have to be passed on by the publisher to wholesalers, retailers and consumers.

Most countries in the EU (but not the UK) allow imports and exports of books free of VAT but charge it on books delivered in the country of manufacture. For example, if a UK publisher prints a German edition at a German printer then VAT will be levied. It is possible (but time consuming) to recover the VAT paid if arrangements are made in advance.

UK VAT is payable on components of books (e.g. film, jackets, printed sheets) invoiced separately, but this can normally be reclaimed by the publisher. However, most printers will include these items in their overall invoice for the book, which will not be VAT-able.

Paper orders

Where the publisher is supplying paper, orders to paper merchants should contain the following information:

- type of paper;
- quantity in sheets or metres for reels;
- size of sheet or reel;
- grammage;
- grain direction of sheets;
- printing process and method of binding if unsewn;
- preferred moisture content;
- whether precision trimmed or guillotined, or reel tolerance;
- packing and delivery details.

Electronic ordering

Instead of orders sent on paper or by email, many printers now offer the publisher the ability to input orders directly into the printer's MIS (Management Information System) or the publisher may have electronic ordering as part of their own system.

7
CO-EDITIONS

Introduction

This is where a book has been designed so that a change to another language affects only the black plates. Typically the way this works is that the first run will consist of the English languages i.e. the UK edition, US edition (with a full language change between them) and Australian and Canadian editions, which may only have imprint changes (see below). Then a few months later there will be a co-edition run consisting of a number of different languages in the same run, and in which the colour plates will remain the same but the black text plate will change. Sometimes the foreign language editions will be produced on the same print run as the English edition, but this can be difficult to schedule because of the time needed for translation.

The cost of plates and make-ready for this black plate

change is far less than changing all four plates, and the initial set-up cost can therefore be spread over all the editions being printed. Co-editions are particularly common for illustrated children's books and highly illustrated cookery and coffee-table books.

Pre-planning

When the publisher has a title for which they hope to sell co-editions, the editorial and design work has to be done in such a way that all type is in black only, set up on a separate layer inside the file, so that a foreign language edition can be produced by changing only the black plate. This means no type can be used in the images or in colour and no type can be reversed out of colour.

It is possible to have type reversed out of black, but this needs to be set up in such a way that the black background that touches the images is part of the image layer and not part of the text layer in the file.

The exception to this rule is usually the jacket or cover, where to require only a black-plate change would be too restrictive on the design. Most co-editions allow for the foreign publisher to change all four colours on the jacket or cover.

One thing to bear in mind is that, particularly with children's books, the illustrations should not be too specific to the originating country. An example would be double-decker buses, which we have in the UK but are rare in other countries, so the publisher might use a single-decker 'generic' bus instead.

The originating publisher will obviously need to have

cleared rights (for text and illustrations) for all the countries to whom they are selling.

Estimating

The Foreign Sales department will ask for prices for various quantities/countries for the co-editions. Production will ask the printer for the following prices:

- Printing cost for original (UK) printing;
- Run-on cost (i.e. cost of extra copies printed at the same time);
- Cost of a black language change to all text pages;
- Cost of a four-colour cover/jacket change as well as any changes to cover/jacket finishes such as foil blocking/embossing/spot UV;
- Cost of change to the blocking brass on the spine;
- Cost of freight to the various countries;
- Costs for individual extras such as individual shrink-wrapping;
- Cost savings if the co-editions were to take a simplified version, e.g. a PLC with no jacket; no head and tail bands; ends unprinted; using a lighter text paper.

There are areas that can incur extra costs and may cause problems if they are not specified in advance. They are:

- An allowance for advance copies, and the courier

costs for these, sent to each co-edition partner plus
to the main UK publisher;

- Courier costs for plotter proofs to be sent to each
co-edition publisher. Some UK publishers also
order an extra set of plotter proofs so that they
can check that the co-edition text is falling in
the correct places and not affecting the colour
elements;

- The packing and shipping elements included in
the basic price so that Foreign Sales can advise its
customers. Many co-edition publishers have their
own specific packing and shipping requirements,
e.g. cartons of a specific size, particular types of
pallets, etc.

Production can then quote these prices to Foreign Sales which
will add on a figure representing a share of the editorial, design
and reproduction costs, profit, and the author or illustrator's
royalty (if any). This royalty is usually a percentage of receipts
rather than a percentage of the retail price.

Schedule

This will have the following information:

- Date when the originating publisher supplies the application files;
- Date for PDFs from the foreign publisher;
- Date for plotter proofs;
- Date for approval of plotter proofs;
- Despatch date;
- Delivery date.

If the application files are sent out to the co-edition publishers before the first (English) edition is finalized, this can create a number of complications as any further changes that are made to the first edition need to be communicated to the co-edition publishers. If any changes are made that mean the colour is moved in any way, the co-edition publishers would then need to be supplied with replacement layout files for those specific pages.

The main scheduling problems for co-editions are ensuring that the files for all the editions arrive on time and that all editions return their plotter proofs on time. The costs are based on all printing together and if one of the co-edition publishers misses the date not only will it increase the cost of their edition but it also affects the costs of the others, which are based on the start-up costs being spread over the total quantity being printed. A missed date puts the originating publisher in a difficult position, as they are contracted to supply the other co-edition publishers' books at a set price on a set date. If the offending publisher is so late that the others have to go ahead without them, it is possible to print that publisher's sheets without the text and go back to press later – but this is a lot more expensive than co-printing.

If one of the co-edition publishers makes very heavy corrections at plotter proof stage, this can incur extra costs and delay the schedule. It is useful to specify how fast the co-publishers are expected to check and return their plotter proofs and also to specify that if more than, say, ten pages are corrected then the publisher will be charged a correction fee per page. This discourages heavy changes.

Co-edition publisher's purchase order

When the price and schedule have been agreed, the foreign publisher supplies a purchase order giving the quantity, delivery date, packing and shipping details and advance copy requirements. Production then incorporates this information in the printing and binding order covering all the editions.

Supplying files

The originating publisher will supply application files (Quark or InDesign), detailed instructions to the foreign publisher listing the fonts they have used and the instructions for working on the files (reminding the co-edition publishers not to move any of the colour elements) and making the print-ready PDFs. They will also sometimes specify the flight-checks that they are expected to run on their PDFs. The text will be set up on a separate layer and the lower layer – with the colour elements – will be locked down. The foreign publisher will then use this layer as a template for the foreign-language text, ensuring that they fit their text into the boxes provided. The co-edition publishers supply the originating publisher composite black text-only PDFs as single pages (not spreads). Some publishers and printers require that these should be accompanied by a print-out. Where the cover/jacket has all four colours changed, the foreign publisher should supply a colour digital proof with the complete PDF.

When the foreign publisher supplies a PDF of their black text it is sent to the originating publisher, who sends it to the printer. Some publishers encourage their co-edition publishers to supply their PDF files directly to the printer as this can shorten the schedules. The printer supplies either a physical plotter proof (which will show the foreign language and all the illustrations in colour) or an emailed version of this. The plotter proof is not for checking the colour quality, but for checking the content and the positioning of the text and colour. The colour quality of the original edition is checked on colour digital proofs by the original publisher. Where the jacket or cover has all colours changed, the printer should supply a digital proof (if the foreign publisher has not provided one with the PDFs).

Despatch and delivery

When Production receives the despatch details with the final quantity, it advises the foreign publisher of these details and Foreign Sales then invoices the foreign publisher for the books.

Imprint changes

This is where there is another English language edition printed at the same time as the publisher's original edition. This might be for a US or Australian publisher or UK book club or direct market client. It could also be for a US edition where Americanization of the text is not required. Normally, the imprint change will be to the title page and imprint (copyright) page, as well as the cover or jacket and spine brass for a hardback. This is much cheaper than a full co-edition with a language change, as the text-plate alteration is only to two black plates, rather than all the black plates in the book. Sometimes the design requires that all four colours have to be changed on the cover or jacket.

8
TECHNICAL DEVELOPMENTS

Introduction

The production controller must have good technical knowledge of all the processes involved in book production. Because the technology is changing constantly and rapidly, production staff must ensure that they keep abreast of these changes. The purpose of this is twofold – as well as needing to be up to date to be able to handle their own work effectively, Production also has a duty to keep colleagues in other departments informed of technical developments that will impact on their work.

E-books

At the time of writing (2012), a tipping point in the balance between e-books and their printed equivalents has been reached. Amazon are already selling more e-books than physical hardbacks and paperbacks combined and the larger publishers are predicting that e-books will represent more than 50% of their turnover in five to ten years' time. This will obviously have implications for book printers and publishers' production departments. We are already seeing a reduction in the quantities of physical books sold and therefore a consequent reduction in the quantities of books produced (particularly black-and-white text-only books such as novels). In response to this, the larger book printers, both in the UK and abroad, are cutting back their investments in printing and binding machinery designed for longer runs and, instead, investing in equipment suitable for much shorter runs. This is usually digital printing equipment (see below).

Most publishers (particularly the larger firms) have set up separate digital departments and often these will handle all aspects of the creation of e-books and apps, without the involvement of Production. This inevitably means that production departments will become smaller and therefore the job opportunities and promotions will be restricted in traditional publishing. An obvious answer to this is for those who are considering a career in Production to equip themselves with the skills to work in the digital areas of publishing, and in particular with an understanding of the conversion of files to e-book formats and an ability to oversee the whole administration of a company's e-book programme.

However, we are not about to see the death of the printed

book. Although titles such as novels and biographies lend themselves to e-book publication, there are several categories of book which do not. Examples of these include cookery books, illustrated children's books and those intended as gifts, where the buyer wants to give a physical object rather than a download token.

MAKING E-BOOK FILES

In order to publish the e-book, the text has to be converted into a mobi file for Amazon and, usually, an ePub file for other etailers. In some publishing houses, this conversion is organized by Editorial or Design, but it can be Production that does this. Until recently, it was achieved by converting the PDF used for printing, but the latest versions of Adobe InDesign (5.5) and QuarkXPress (9) enable exporting direct to ePub files with reflowable text (required, as e-books have a function that enables the type to be enlarged or reduced, meaning that the original line endings in the print PDF no longer apply). The ePub file has XHTML content, which can be further edited if required. The mobi file required for the Amazon Kindle can then be converted from the ePub file.

Backlist titles, for which only a print PDF exists and no application files, can be converted to ePub and mobi files by specialist digitizing houses. Here, the file conversion often needs manual intervention, particularly when there are pictures or tables in the book. It is important to realize that it is not just a question of pressing a button and expecting software to perform the conversion.

Usually, the ePub and mobi files enable clicking on content and index entries to move to the relevant page of the book.

Video and audio can now be included in ePub files. Whether files are made from the applications or PDFs, they need to be proofread, as glitches can occur in the conversion process.

Other considerations are that each e-book should have a different ISBN from the printed version, with separate ISBNs for ePub and mobi versions. When proofread and approved, the e-book files then have to be uploaded to the etailers, following their detailed instructions. Sometimes the e-book will have a different – often typographical – cover to the printed version, because the publisher doesn't wish to pay extra for rights to use the cover image or design on the printed book. Books that have illustrations in the printed version may be published without them as e-books, again because of the additional rights costs.

APPS

These are applications for use on iPhones, iPads or Android mobile devices. In the case of books, the text is enhanced with elements that don't appear in the printed book. These can include video, audio, photographs and interactive elements. Apps are usually created by specialist software developers. The cost of creating apps can be very high, so the expected sales quantity needs to be able to cover this fixed cost.

ILLUSTRATED BOOKS

Books with integrated illustrations may not lend themselves to conversion to ePub or mobi files and many devices don't support colour in any case. However, they can be supplied as

PDFs retaining the layout of the original printed book. This applies particularly to illustrated children's books. Recent developments in e-book creation have seen a divergence from standards. Apple was the first to launch an extension to the format to allow for 'PDF-like' layouts from an ePub file, with fixed position text and the integration of video, audio, simple interactivity and complex imagery. Amazon followed with a format based on HTML5 called the KF8 standard, which, while functionally identical to the Apple 'Fixed Layout' format, differs in the type of coding it requires. The latest development in this field happened in February 2012 when Apple launched the free iBooks Author application. This produces a format based on ePub3, designed for highly interactive textbooks on the iPad.

E-BOOK COSTS

An example of the basic costs of an e-book is shown below. They differ from that of a physical book because they include VAT and the author royalties are a higher percentage (25% or often more). In addition, the publisher has no production costs apart from the minimal cost of making the e-book file and proofreading it.

> Retail price £4.99
> VAT 83p
> Etailer discount 55% = £2.29
> Author's royalty of 25% of receipts = 47p
> Margin to include overheads = £1.40

Note that there are no fixed costs, such as Editorial, given here, as it is assumed that these were recovered on the printed edition. They would have to be added if it were a stand-alone e-book. One joy of e-books is that there are no returns!

Digital printing

Although most books are printed by the offset lithography process, increasingly digital printing is being used. Developments in digital presses mean that they can now be economical for runs of up to 2,000 copies. This will only increase, meaning that in the future conventional offset litho will only be used for longer runs.

A digital press works rather like an office ink-jet or laser printer in that the PDF is sent to the print engine and does not require a metal plate to be made. This means that the start-up costs are minimal, which is what makes the process competitive for short runs. Most digital book presses print all the pages in sequence, rather than printing a fixed number of pages like 64 or 96. Often the binding line is linked to the printing press, so that a book is printed and bound in one operation. Most digitally printed books are bound unsewn or notch – not only for cost reasons but also because where binding is linked to printing the pages come off the press in units unsuitable for sewn binding (e.g. as four-page sections).

Quality was not very good on earlier digital presses, particularly when using halftones and tints, but is now improving and becoming indistinguishable from offset.

PRINT ON DEMAND

Digital printing has enabled print on demand (POD), where the publisher keeps no stock in the warehouse and single copies are printed in response to a customer order and despatched within two or three days. The main advantage is that the publisher does not have to carry stock, which may mean tying up the investment for years and incurring storage costs. Before short runs or POD were possible, a publisher might print 1,000 copies, sell quite a few on first publication, go out of stock, and often then let the book go out of print as small volumes would be too expensive to reprint.

The POD or short-run book printed digitally will always be costlier than a book with a run of 2,000 or more, but the editorial and design costs are amortized on the first run so that a short-run reprint still yields a profit. Short-run hardback books tend to be expensive so most POD or short-run books are paperbacks, even if the original first printing was hardback.

The sort of books which lend themselves particularly to short-run or POD are academic or legal books which might sell at £15 to £25 and can withstand a fairly high unit cost.

Digital printing is also used for self-publishing, where an individual can get a book printed and arrange for it to be sold on Amazon and via other retailers. Until recently, digital printing was only economical for black-and-white books, but developments in digital presses have meant that increasingly it is possible to print shorter runs of colour books.

With such short-runs, it is vital that estimating and order processing is all handled via an IT system, otherwise the overheads would be crippling. Estimates are usually provided as a price scale, often using Excel, so that the publisher can feed in the specification and quantity and get a unit price.

ADVANCE PROOFS

Digital printing is also used for advance book proofs, where the publisher prints a short run (e.g. 150 copies) of the book at uncorrected proof stage and sends it out for review and publicity several months before printing the main run. Colour digital printing can be used for blads (book layout and design) that might be sixteen pages of content from the book wire-stitched into a cover – again, these are used for advance publicity. Digital colour printing has made colour blads much more affordable than when printed by offset.

Keeping informed

Such rapid technical advances make it imperative that the production controller and manager keep themselves up to date. Normally, it will be the production manager or director who will inform themselves of developments and pass them on to their staff. The sources of this information are:

- the *trade press:* specialist printing periodicals such as *PrintWeek* carry items on the latest technical developments;
- *training:* courses at Publishing Training Centre, Imago Publishing and colleges of printing;
- *trade shows:* exhibitions such as IPEX show all the latest equipment;
- *visits to suppliers and manufacturers:* this is probably the most useful source of information on new

techniques, because it can be related to the type of work produced by the publisher.

Informing colleagues

As the department in closest touch with these new techniques, it is Production's responsibility to keep colleagues in other departments informed of developments that can affect the way they do their work. For example, the possibility of economically producing short-run books could mean that the publisher considers issuing titles that would previously have been uneconomical.

This information can be passed on in an informal way as part of day-to-day contacts with other departments; by circulating copies of relevant articles in trade journals; or by organizing in-house seminars with outside speakers where necessary.

Conclusion

Technology is breaking down the divisions between departments, and Production has a key role in helping a company to make the most effective use of all the improvements in book production methods.

9

QUALITY CONTROL

Introduction

Production is responsible for the quality of the finished product, and this is achieved by applying quality standards at various stages in the production of a book.

Quality control starts with the choice of supplier (*see* Print and paper buying, p.38). The production controller will want to see samples and possibly visit the plant before taking on a new supplier in order to establish that the supplier is capable of producing the standard of quality required, by virtue of the equipment they possess and the work they have done for other publishers.

Quality is also affected by the choice of materials. If you are using materials – papers or cover weights – that you are not familiar with, it is important to obtain an accurate dummy before confirming the order. If you are choosing an uncoated paper because it will give you a better bulk for the same price, then it is important that you see what some of your colour images will look like on that paper.

Reproduction and proofing

The technical developments of recent years have completely changed the way that the quality of black-and-white and colour images are assessed. Colour images were usually supplied as transparencies. It was the job of the repro house to match the transparency as closely as possible when proofing, and for the proof to then be checked by Production and Design and corrected and reproofed if necessary. Instead, the images are now often supplied to Production as digital files, which are either photographs taken on digital cameras or scans (usually produced by the designer).

In many companies, the designer supplies PDFs to Production, which then obtains digital colour proofs calibrated to an agreed standard (e.g. Fogra 39L [ISO 12647 – 2:2004], the current European standard). When proofing, the repro house or printer are making the proof of the file automatically (to the agreed standard), so are not altering the colour values of the file supplied to them. This means that if the publisher is unhappy with the colours on the proof, it is up to the designer to alter the file (usually by retouching in Photoshop) and then send it for revised proofing. Working this way makes colour quality an in-house responsibility (or that of a freelance designer commissioned by Editorial or Design), rather than that of an outside supplier. Another option when an image is sub-standard is to find a suitable replacement image with better colour values.

The images should ideally be sharp and have an original minimum resolution of 300dpi in the size at which it will be printed. When the image is being enlarged, the resolution needs to be proportionately higher – so where an image is appearing at twice the size of the original, it will need to be 600dpi. This is not a hard and fast rule, as often it is not possible to obtain 300dpi original files and adequate results can be obtained from lower resolution files, although these should be proofed to check the quality.

It is possible to increase the resolution in Photoshop through resampling – sometimes called false resolution. This means you create extra pixels, but not extra detail. The software creates pixels by averaging out the detail from the surrounding pixels. This way you can theoretically create a 300dpi image from one of 72dpi, but it would still be just a low-resolution image that would not look at all good when printed. This is why the image quality needs to be checked at 100% in Photoshop – a check usually done by the designer, but in some companies by Production or an outside repro house.

At the high end of the market, for art and museum books, well-known photographers or well-known children's illustrators, publishers are still using repro houses to process the images. Here highly skilled technicians retouch and adjust the images in Photoshop, so that once they are converted to CMYK they will produce a close match to the digital image. They also insert 'unsharp masking' into the images, which always gives a printed image a sharper look but needs to be done at the last stage, once the image size and the paper type is known, as it affects the settings used.

It would usually be up to Production to arrange this repro house work. The repro house supply proofs – normally digital – for the publisher to check. If the reproduction and colour values are not as expected the repro house will supply further rounds of proofs until they are correct.

Printing

Very few books are now seen on press by the publisher. The printer's job is to match the digital proofs and files submitted. However, the printer will only get a close match to the colour proofs if they have been proofed to the appropriate standard (e.g. Fogra 39 for coated matt papers) and if the files have been correctly made. If this has been properly done then, with the modern presses most printers are now using, the printer usually gets a very good match to the proofs without requiring the publisher to approve the result on press. Tracking, however, can still create colour problems as sometimes the images that run in the same ink track (see below) can require very different amounts of ink. It is then up to the printer to decide how to balance out the images so that they get the best result overall.

Occasionally for major titles with very long runs, or titles where colour is particularly critical, such as books reproducing works of art, a publisher will decide to pass on press. This is normally the responsibility of Production, but sometimes a designer or editor will also attend.

It is important to approach press passes with the right attitude, which does not mean telling the machine minder how to do the job but is more a question of interpretation: does the publisher want a bright, sparkly result or a more subtle one? Sometimes it is a matter of indicating to the minder what the publisher sees as the more important images, or areas of colour. The inks can be adjusted to a certain extent still keeping to accepted trade ink tolerances. At this stage the printer is not altering anything in the publisher's PDF files – just changing the dot gain or ink balance on press.

When passing on press, first check the printed sheet against the plotter proof to ensure that all corrections marked on the plotter have been carried out, then check the sheet for spots, which can be caused by dust in the platemaking process. Finally, check the colour values against the digital proofs and the register (the accurate positioning of the plates).

The ink is rolled in the short direction of the sheet, so that if colour is altered in one area then all the other subjects in that area ('track') across the whole width of the sheet will show that colour alteration. This means that often a compromise has to be reached. For example, if a subject is lacking in yellow, then increasing this colour will mean an increase for all the subjects in that track, possibly making some too yellow. Double-page spreads need to be checked carefully because, owing to the imposition, the two pages may not be adjacent on the printed sheet and may even be on different sheets (where the left-hand page is the last page of one section and the right-hand page the first page of the next). One of the pages should be cut out of the sheet and laid next to its companion to check for even colour across the spread. The printed sheet should be viewed in standard lighting conditions.

Where the book is not seen on press, the publisher can ask

to see running sheets or F&Gs (folded and gathered sections) before it is bound and check them in the office.

Binding

Most binding faults are self-evident from the advance copies and the next step is to establish whether they occur throughout the run. The way to do this is to check a random sample, such as one copy from each of three parcels taken from different layers of each pallet. If the problem occurs in more than one part of the stock then the whole run will have to be checked, either at the warehouse or after returning the books to the binder.

Some binders have special equipment to check the strength of binding, particularly for unsewn binding, such as page-pull or flex-strength machines that check the strength of the adhesive bond.

Repairs

Where some or all of the copies of a title are found to be faulty, it may be possible to repair them to avoid having to reprint the book. Often the printer can perform these repairs or a repair job can be placed by the printer or publisher with one of several UK companies who specialize in handwork and repairs. Here are some examples of the type of repairs that can be carried out:

- Faulty jackets can be removed and books re-jacketed by hand with the reprinted jacket;

- A page which contains an error can be replaced with a two-page cancel. Here the offending page is removed neatly, leaving a 3mm strip onto which is glued a replacement page. This can be done neatly enough so as not to be noticeable;

- A wrong price on a cover or jacket can be over-stickered or screen-printed to correct it.;

- Where there is a fault on a paperback cover, the book can be stripped and rebound. This consists of cutting the backs off the books, removing the covers by hand and then rebinding with a new cover. This method results in a slightly smaller book as it is retrimmed – losing between 3 and 6mm in height or width. This may mean that where a book bleeds, some of the image is lost or that the margins become too small.

These are just examples and there are many other ways of repairing books. Most methods are expensive, but may be cheaper than doing a complete reprint.

Rejecting a book

This is sometimes necessary, but should not be done lightly. Rather than being the decision of just Production or the designer, senior sales representatives should also be involved, as it will have an impact on the delivery date. Sometimes the designer or production controller is too close to the job, having worked for months on a particular book. It is worth having the dispassionate view of the sales director or manager as to whether the book is really not sales-worthy for the particular market or client. It is not easy to reject a book that is of a slightly worse quality than the proofs – it normally has to be seen as seriously substandard. If you are disappointed in the quality this is something you should remember when next placing a book with your choice of supplier or could use as a way of bargaining down a future price.

Reviewing quality with colleagues

It can be useful to take a month's titles to a progress meeting to discuss the comparative quality of each. This might also be the occasion to look at design, and also to consider whether the specifications are right for books of that type or whether they need to be revised for similar titles in the future.

10

PRODUCTION AND THE ENVIRONMENT

Introduction

Every industry and individual now considers the impact their activities have on the environment, and book publishing is no exception. The production of books can have major environmental impacts and publishers, printers and papermakers are working together to minimize the effect their activities have on the world.

Paper

The publishing, printing and papermaking industries have come together to try to ensure that paper and board used is legally harvested from sustainable forests and from non-controversial sources. Sustainable forestry means not contributing to the depletion of the world's forests and that trees used in papermaking are replaced, often with two or three trees planted for every one cut down.

In some parts of the world the mills are less concerned about these environmental issues and some of their papers use pulp from old conservation value forestry that should not have been destroyed.

Two organizations have been set up to promote responsible forest management – the Forest Stewardship Council (FSC) and the Programme for Endorsement of Forest Certification (PEFC). These schemes accredit companies in the paper supply chain – forest owners, papermakers and printers – so that the end user knows that all the parties involved can prove that the source of the wood used is a legally harvested, sustainable and well-managed forest.

Both schemes also aim at promoting economic, social and environmental management of the forests. The FSC criteria are more stringent than those for PEFC and it is considered 'best practice' to use FSC papers where possible. However as only 9% of forests worldwide fall under either scheme there is a shortage of this paper worldwide. A book printed on FSC or PEFC paper can carry the relevant logo on the cover or copyright page. Now, most UK book printers are FSC and PEFC accredited and much uncoated paper used for book printing in the UK is FSC or PEFC accredited. However, many grades of coated paper (particularly those sourced in the Far East) are not accredited under either scheme.

Being able to show that their books are not in any way contributing to the deforestation of the world – the destruction of primary forests, the endangering of species, the harming of indigenous people dependant on the forest for their survival – or to climate change, has become an important consideration for many publishers. To help deal with this problem, PREPS was set up – a group started in the UK made up of twenty-three leading publishers, who have come together to develop an understanding of a responsible paper supply chain. Paper information is gathered and graded based on the forest source information, with a Grade of 1, 3 or 5. Grade 5 is recycled, FSC or 100% PEFC certified paper. Grade 3 is from known and responsible sources and Grade 1 is from unknown or high-risk sources. This means that PREPS Grade 3 papers while not being FSC or PEFC accredited are from known and responsible sources. Many publishers are now only using papers that are either certified FSC or PEFC, or papers that are PREPS Grade 3. Web links for FSC, PEFC and PREPS are on pp.139 and 140.

RECYCLED PAPER

This contains a percentage of fibres made from waste paper. Environmental pressures have resulted in a big increase in the amount of recycled paper produced in recent years. Recycling paper means that waste paper is re-used rather than disposed of in landfill sites or incinerators and also obviously reduces the number of trees required. It also uses less water and energy in the papermaking process.

Recycled paper is suitable for newsprint (which is often 100% recycled), but for book papers too high a percentage of recycled pulp will give problems with whiteness and stiffness. The publisher may not always be able to find a recycled paper with the right price and quality, but recycled papers are improving all the time.

Paper mills are making efforts to reduce their environmental impacts in other ways – papermaking uses a tremendous amount of energy and mills are starting to use alternative sources of power, such as biogas and wind. Paper mills are also trying to reduce the amount of toxic by-products and their use of water by operating a closed system.

Ink

There are also environmental impacts to consider in the manufacture of ink. Producers are now using renewable sources such as vegetable oils or soy, rather than mineral oils, and printers are using water-based inks where possible instead of those with a solvent base.

Printing

Printers also play their part in helping the environment with recycling of waste paper and ink, alternative energy sources and printing using alcohol-free damping and waterless offset.

Working conditions

Environmental issues also include the human impacts of working methods. Most large multinational companies have codes of conduct for their suppliers, covering health and safety, hours of work, trades union recognition, and so on. These are used in particular in developing countries, to ensure that printing factories have good working conditions and employment practices. These codes of conduct are backed up with regular inspections to ensure compliance.

Many of the third-party clients of publishers (both in the UK and abroad), such as large store chains, insist that the printers used for their books are signed up to a code of conduct and may refuse to place an order with a publisher if the printer is not accredited.

Safety

Children's books and books plus (novelty books) are covered by safety legislation in many countries, including Europe and the USA. In Europe there is the European Toy Safety Directive and there is similar legislation in the USA. This means that many children's books and particularly those with a novelty element, such as an attached toy, have to be safety tested, which can be an expensive and time-consuming process. Tests include toxicity, choking hazard, flammability, lead content, phthalate content and electrical toy safety.

This is a complex area, with the legislation changing

from time to time, so production controllers (particularly for children's books) need to keep themselves up-to-date. Training in safety requirements is available and the major Far East suppliers of children's books will be able to advise what is needed to comply with the legislation.

Conclusion

All of the suppliers involved in book production are now making it a priority to reduce their environmental impacts and will continue to do so in the future.

11
ORGANIZING
YOUR WORK

Introduction

The day-to-day work in the production department consists of small jobs on many different titles, and the constant juggling of priorities. Attention to detail is vital, as is the need for decisions to be recorded in writing (either on paper or electronically). This means that production controllers must learn how to manage time, and to use and develop systems to manage their work efficiently.

Time management

At any given time a production controller will have many jobs to be done, some of which are more urgent than others, for example:

- *Immediate*: PDFs or proofs to be sent to suppliers or internal departments; estimates required for a meeting the next day; orders that have to be done to enable the supplier to order material;

- *Medium-term*: estimates for projects; checking invoices; selecting the suppliers for a book;

- *Long-term*: keeping up-to-date with technical developments; developing new systems for handling production work.

It is difficult to keep the correct balance between these categories of work, and the danger is that the 'immediate' items will eclipse the medium- and long-term work. The way to resolve this problem is to have target dates for completing the longer-term work, and, where these dates are looming, to look closely at the short-term work and see if it all needs doing that day, or whether it can be left for a day or two to enable the medium- and long-term work to be done in time.

A useful discipline is to do first whatever is holding up the work of others. For example, unless you return a proof the supplier cannot take the work to the next stage; if invoices are not approved then the accounts department can't pay them; if an estimate is not done then the quantity cannot be decided.

Materials in and out

A significant part of Production's work is receiving and sending material such as PDFs and proofs to and from suppliers and internal departments. It is important that records of material in and out are kept in writing. Material should be accompanied by a letter or memo listing what is enclosed and the next stage required with the date needed. Where originals are enclosed, these should be counted by Production and also by the party (be it a supplier or internal department) sending the material to Production – if this is not done and a valuable original is lost it will not be possible to establish where it was lost and thus who is responsible.

Forms

As discussed elsewhere, Production will have forms (either paper or electronic) for specifications, estimates, costing, printing orders, etc., and these should be reviewed from time to time with colleagues in other departments to check their relevance and usefulness.

Emails

Emails are the usual method of communication with outside suppliers and internal departments. Email is instant, provides a record in writing and has transformed work in the modern office. However, there are disadvantages when email is misused. A common fault is to copy in individuals who do not really need to see the message , thereby filling up their inboxes unnecessarily. When doing another task, it is tempting to pause to open an incoming email, thus breaking concentration – most emails can wait an hour or so before requiring a response. Another common fault is to only respond to part of an email, meaning that the sender has to write another email requesting the missing information. It is helpful to have an email signature containing your phone number(s) and postal address. Sometimes, senders forward the complete conversation thread with each email – it is better just to include the previous email, rather than the whole correspondence.

Management information systems (MIS)

As mentioned earlier (*see* pp.76 and 87), some printers open these up to publishers, meaning that communication of information (e.g. dates/quantities) can be inputted directly, without having to send a separate email request to the printer. This saves time and double handling and reduces errors.

Meetings

Publishers hold regular progress and price-fixing meetings, and the format and purpose of these should be examined periodically – for example, putting information on a company-wide computer database may reduce their need. Meetings can often eat into productive time, so the number of people at a meeting and its length should always be minimized. The role of any 'observers', rather than active participants, in meetings should be critically examined, as should the frequency of meetings.

Statistics

Production should be able to compile statistics such as the number of titles produced in different categories, the volume and value of work at individual suppliers, average run lengths, etc. These are needed to help make meaningful decisions about the placing of work and can be of use to other departments. They also show the workload of Production and enable comparisons to be made with previous years.

Filing

Some publishers now file everything electronically, but whether on paper or electronically, filing should be kept up to date and easily accessible. Filing is a 'medium-term' job, but if it is not done reasonably quickly it will build up and time may be wasted because it will become difficult to find things. When a title is completed the file should be reduced to essential items before being archived.

12

WORKING WITH COLLEAGUES

Introduction

Publishing, probably more than most industries, demands teamwork to succeed. A publishing house is made up of specialists in various disciplines, and their work has to be harnessed towards common objectives. To achieve teamwork, the barriers between departments must be broken down, and the staff of one department should be sensitive to the needs and aims of others.

Sometimes this can be helped by an organization being structured so that it is split into divisions (often imprints), each made up of a team of people from different disciplines. The idea is that a member of the division will identify with that division, rather than the production, editorial or design department. However, even where companies are organized as departments rather than divisions, it should be possible to avoid disputes based on 'territory' rather than the facts of a particular issue.

Status of Production

The status of the production department varies greatly from one company to another. In some cases, Production is seen as a 'service' department to be subservient to, and carry out the wishes of, other departments such as Editorial. Elsewhere, Production can be too powerful and lay the dead hand of bureaucracy on the efforts of editors and designers.

What is needed is balance, where the company appreciates the responsibility Production has in being the largest-spending department, but does not allow Production to use that fact for its own convenience rather than acting as a partner working to a common objective with other departments. Production's status should be equal to that of the other main departments.

Editors

The commissioning editor, in deciding which books to publish, has a key role in the company's profitability and needs the support of Production to supply estimates in time to do deals with authors, to make books viable by good print buying and to keep Editorial up to date on technical developments that could offer new publishing opportunities.

Production has to work closely with copy-editors to achieve schedules, and a good relationship will mean that there will be 'give and take' and an effective flow of information.

Production should not be seen to be obstructive, but should try to be genuinely helpful when problems arise on schedules and prices.

Designers

A designer will, rightly, consider the final look of the book to be the most important criterion, whereas Production is also concerned with cost and timing. A good relationship between Design and Production results from a reasonable compromise between these differing objectives: a book winning a design award loses some of its glory if it costs far more than planned and is delivered late, while the look of a book can sometimes be badly spoilt by a 'penny-pinching' response from Production to a designer's entirely reasonable request for an enhancement to the specification.

Even more than with Editorial, there is a need for

Production to provide Design with technical advice and to supply information about technical developments.

Sales/marketing

As well as delivering the books on time, Production has to be aware of Sales's need for advance material such as jackets for publicity and information for booksellers. Production can sometimes be guilty of thinking in terms of schedules only in so far as the final delivery date is met, rather than realizing the importance of timely publicity material.

The sales of a book depend partly on its price, which results from the specification and buying done by Production, and Production must work with Sales to ensure that a book is not under- or over-specified for the market at which it is aimed.

Finance

The Finance or Accounts department needs financial information on time and in the right form to be able to do its job properly – budgets cannot be done without estimates, and accounts cannot be completed if the costings are not up to date.

Production also needs the help of Finance in, for example, paying suppliers on time, which helps to maintain a good relationship with the supplier. The two departments also need to work closely together where using foreign printers and deciding methods of payment or buying currency forward.

Distribution

The warehouse is usually in a different location to the production department, making it more difficult to establish a good working relationship. This can be overcome by production staff visiting the warehouse from time to time.

Production needs to appreciate the importance of meeting the warehouse's packing and delivery requirements. A load delivered on the wrong pallets may involve removing all the parcels by hand and restacking them on new pallets, or may even simply be turned back by the warehouse. It is equally important that paperwork such as delivery notes is presented in the right form. Most warehouses require deliveries to be 'booked in' for a certain time slot. This is to avoid several trucks arriving simultaneously and some having to wait a long time to be unloaded. The warehouse may turn away a delivery if it arrives significantly outside the agreed time slot.

Conclusion

Although Production is not just a service department, one of its functions is to provide a good service to other departments and to be helpful rather than obstructive. It can be too easy for Production to become bureaucratic and hide behind schedules and estimates, rather than actively trying to help other departments achieve their objectives.

It is important that Production is seen to be 'pro-active' in making things happen, rather than just being 'reactive'.

13

WORKING
WITH
SUPPLIERS

Introduction

Good relationships with suppliers are essential to achieve
Production's objectives, and need to be worked at by both
parties. The goal should be a 'partnership' with common
objectives, rather than a contest between adversaries. Good
relationships take time to develop, and this can only happen
if there is continuity. If a publisher uses too many suppliers
for the volume of work, or is always trying out new suppliers,

then inevitably it will not be possible to develop good working relationships.

Establishing a working relationship

This will start with the initial contact, usually from the printer's salesperson, and discussions on whether the printer has the capability to work for the publisher. After estimating and possibly following a visit to the plant, if a printer starts working for a publisher then they will get to know each other's internal staff and methods of working. Each party will therefore have a better idea of what they can do for the other and be able to anticipate the other's requirements.

The relationship may be deepened by working together on a contractual basis, possibly using price scales with a guaranteed volume of work, and can then develop to the stage where the printer considers the publisher's requirements when investing in new equipment. This said it may, however, be unwise for any one printer to do too large a proportion of a publisher's work, or vice versa. Production should always have alternative suppliers available in the case of a supplier giving problems on quality, price or service; so 'exclusivity', although justified in some circumstances, can be unhealthy.

Let's look at the areas of price, quality and service in relationships with suppliers:

- Prices can be reduced where a large volume of work is being placed. As well as savings in the purchase of materials, there are overhead savings in having fewer clients to deal with for a given volume of work.

- A supplier will get to know the publisher's quality standards, and this can be conveyed to the workforce where regular work is placed.

- In terms of service, placing a high volume of work with one supplier enables the publisher to improve the delivery of some titles by postponing other, less urgent ones. Over a period of time the publisher will learn that they can trust the date information given. Printers will also become familiar with the publisher's requirements for information, advance copies and deliveries.

Ethics

As in other areas of business life, ethical standards should be applied when dealing with suppliers. These can cover areas such as confidentiality: it is not ethical to pass information to a supplier's competitor if it has been given in confidence, and, in turn, the supplier should not reveal to a publisher's competitor the fact that they are working on titles that may be competing.

The production controller or manager should not accept valuable gifts or excessive entertaining from a supplier, although having lunch with a supplier can be a good way to get to know them in a less impersonal atmosphere. It is also considered acceptable to receive small gifts from suppliers during the festive season, as tokens of appreciation for work placed during the year.

Probably the main ethical issue between a publisher and supplier is that of *trust*. If one party gives a purely spoken agreement to something then the other party should be able to proceed on that basis, without having to wait for written confirmation. (This in fact is the equivalent of the tacit pledge in the City of London that 'My word is my bond'.)

Disputes

There are bound to be disputes arising with suppliers from time to time and these will test the working relationship between the two parties. An example is where a book is delivered late and misses publication or even incurs penalty charges from a third-party client – normally, the printer will not take responsibility for resulting loss, unless warned in advance of the consequences of late delivery. Another difficult area is where the printing or binding quality is considered sub-standard. Here, the publisher has to persuade the printer that the book is not to standard and then the two parties have to agree how to resolve the problem. If the book is not saleable then it will be rejected (*see* p.112) and reprinted, but in 'borderline' cases the printer may offer a discount.

Disputes such as these are much easier to resolve (often by both parties making a compromise) if there is a good working relationship in the first place. A printer will not want to jeopardize future work by taking an unreasonable stand on a dispute, so usually the two parties manage to reach an acceptable agreement.

Legal considerations

An order placed with a supplier forms a legal contract, where the supplier is agreeing to perform a service in return for payment, and therefore the law of contract applies. Most printers' estimates have 'conditions of trading' printed on the back and it is worth checking these.

Taking legal action is very expensive and time consuming. It very rarely occurs in matters relating to book production, because usually the two parties are able to reach an agreement without reference to the courts. If it is not possible to agree, for example, on whether poor quality justifies a book being rejected and reprinted then the parties may agree to accept the verdict of an independent arbitrator, rather than going to court.

Conclusion

The ability to develop good working relationships with suppliers is an important attribute for a production controller, and helps to ensure that supplier and publisher are working to a common end.

Appendices

Paper usage formulae
To calculate the number of sheets of paper required
to print a book or booklet (excluding covers):

$$\frac{\text{Number of copies to be printed x Number of pages in book}}{\text{Number of pages printing on both sides of sheet}} = \text{Number of sheets required}$$

To calculate the number of copies obtainable from
a given quantity of paper:

$$\frac{\text{Number of sheets x Number of pages printing on both sides of sheet}}{\text{Number of pages in book}} = \text{Number of copies}$$

Bulk calculation for books
In the USA, the bulk of a paper is expressed as a
"bulk factor" that is the number of pages of the
paper that measure one inch thick. The term for
this is PPI (pages per inch). The metric system used
elsewhere, describes bulk with a volume figure that
gives the thickness in millimeters of 200 pages of a
100 gsm paper. The following formulae are used
for metric bulk calculations:

To calculate bulk where the volume of a paper is known:

$$\frac{\text{gsm x volume x half the number of pages}}{10,000} = \text{bulk (mm)}$$

To calculate caliper:

$$\frac{\text{gsm x volume}}{10} = \text{caliper in microns}$$

To calculate volume where caliper and substance
are known:

$$\frac{\text{caliper in microns x 10}}{\text{gsm}} = \text{volume}$$

British standard book sizes		
	mm	inches
A format	178 x 111	7.01 x 4.37
B format	198 x 129	7.80 x 5.08

	Quarto		Octavo	
	mm	inches	mm	inches
Crown	246 x 189	9.69 x 7.44	186 x 123	7.32 x 4.84
Large Crown	258 x 201	10.16 x 7.91	198 x 129	7.8 x 5.08
Demy	276 x 219	10.87 x 8.62	216 x 138	8.5 x 5.43
Royal	312 x 237	12.28 x 9.33	234 x 156	9.21 x 6.14

NB With the exception of A and B format, the above sizes are for sewn books. The unsewn sizes are 3mm (1/8in) narrower to allow for the paper cut off in the unsewn binding process.

Commonly used USA paper sizes:

Legal – 8½ x 14 inches
Foolscap – 8½ x 13 inches
Quarto – 8½ x 11 inches

US book sizes				
	mm	inches	mm	inches
	140 x 216	5½ x 8½	156 x 235	6⅛ x 9¼
	127 x 187	5 x 7⅜	136 x 203	5⅜ x 8
	140 x 210	5½ x 8¼	143 x 213	5⅝ x 8⅜

Conversion tables USA weights to g/m2

In the USA, basis weight is described as the weight of a ream (500 sheets) of paper in one of several standard sizes, depending on the type of work for which the paper is being used. These are:

25 x 38 inches – book (books and general printing)
24 x 36 inches – tag
20 x 26 inches – cover
17 x 22 inches – bond (stationery and forms)

Cover board is also specified by calliper (thickness) rather than weight. The unit used a "point", which is a thousandth of an inch (0.001 inches), so 10 point stock is 0.010 inches thick. Point is abbreviated to "pt.".

500 sheets 25 x 38 inches		500 sheets 24 x 36 inches		500 sheets 20 x 26 inches		500 sheets 17 x 22 inches	
1b	g/m²	1b	g/m²	1b	g/m²	1b	g/m²
20	30	25	41	50	135	8	30
25	31	30	49	55	149	10	38
30	44	35	57	60	162	12	45
35	52	40	65	65	176	14	53
40	59	45	73	70	189	16	60
45	66	50	82	75	203	18	68
50	74	55	90	80	216	20	75
55	81	60	98	85	230	22	83
60	89	65	105	90	243	24	90
65	96	70	114	95	256	26	98
70	104	75	122	100	270	28	105
75	111	80	130	105	284	30	113
80	118	85	138	110	298		
85	126	90	147	115	310		
90	133	95	155	120	324		
95	140	100	163	125	338		
100	148	125	204	130	352		
105	155	150	244	135	366		
110	162	175	285	140	379		
115	170	200	325	145	392		
120	178	225	365	150	405		
125	185	250	400				
130	193	275	450				
135	200	300	490				
140	208						
145	215						
150	222						

Select bibliography

The All New Print Production Handbook, David Bann
(Rotovision, 2011)
Bookmaking Editing/Design/Production, Marshall Lee (W. W.
Norton, 2009)
Book Production, Adrian Bullock (Routledge, 2012)
The Effective Editor's Handbook, Barbara Horn
(Pira International, 1997)
Pocket Pal: A Graphic Arts Production Handbook (Graphic
Arts Technical Foundation, 2007) available from USA
Production for Graphic Designers, Alan Pipes (Laurence King,
2009)

Useful web links

http://www.fsc-uk.org/
The Forest Stewardship Council certifies papers as coming
from sustainable and well-managed sources.

http://www.galleyclub.co.uk/
The Galley Club exists for publishers and book producers to
promote and discuss all aspects of trades and crafts involved
in book publishing. Membership covers the whole spectrum
from publishers, printers, editors, designers, typesetters and

freelancers. The Galley Club meets in London every month from October to June.

http://www.imago.co.uk/
Imago Publishing Limited offer book production services to publishers as well as a range of training courses for production staff. This website also has comprehensive instructions for supplying PDFs.

http://www.pefc.co.uk/
The Programme for Endorsement of Forest Certification certifies papers as coming from sustainable and well-managed sources.

http://prepsgroup.com/
PREPS is a joint initiative from twenty-three leading publishers. These companies have come together to develop their understanding of responsible paper supply chains. The group is supported by a database, which holds technical specifications and details of the pulps and forest sources of the papers they use. It also holds data on CO_2 emissions and water use at the paper mill level. Based on the forest source information, each paper is awarded a grade of 1, 3, or 5 using the PREPS Grading System. This considers the country of origin of the wood fibre and how the forest sources have been managed.

http://www.train4publishing.co.uk/
The Publishing Training Centre offers a wide range of courses for production staff.

http://www.wynkyndeworde.co.uk
The Wynkyn de Worde Society is for people dedicated to excellence in all aspects of printing and the various stages of its creation, production, finishing and dissemination. Since its foundation the society has looked beyond the ever-changing techniques of the world of printing to the proliferating spheres of communication. This it has done chiefly through its main activity, four luncheons a year at Stationers' Hall in London, which are followed by a talk given by an invited speaker.

INDEX

This book was produced by CPI Antony Rowe on an HP
T350 digital press for the text and an HP Indigo 7500 for the
cover. The text paper is Munken Print White 80 gsm vol 18.

CPI Antony Rowe is part of the CPI UK group

CPI Antony Rowe
Bumper's Farm
Chippenham
Wiltshire
SN14 6LH
United Kingdom

Tel: +44 (0)1249 659705
Fax: +44 (0)1249 443103
Email: sales@antonyrowe.co.uk
Website: http://www.cpibooks.com